IT Skills for Successful Study

Visit our free study skills resource at **www.skills4study.com**

Palgrave Study Guides

Authoring a PhD
Career Skills
Critical Thinking Skills
e-Learning Skills
Effective Communication for Arts and
  Humanities Students
Effective Communication for Science and
  Technology
The Foundations of Research
The Good Supervisor
How to Manage your Arts, Humanities and
  Social Science Degree
How to Manage your Distance and Open
  Learning Course
How to Manage your Postgraduate Course
How to Manage your Science and
  Technology Degree
How to Study Foreign Languages
How to Write Better Essays
IT Skills for Successful Study
Making Sense of Statistics
The Mature Student's Guide to Writing
The Postgraduate Research Handbook
Presentation Skills for Students

The Principles of Writing in Psychology
Professional Writing
Research Using IT
Skills for Success
The Student Life Handbook
The Palgrave Student Planner
The Student's Guide to Writing (2nd edn)
The Study Skills Handbook (2nd edn)
Study Skills for Speakers of English as a
  Second Language
Studying the Built Environment
Studying Economics
Studying History (2nd edn)
Studying Mathematics and its Applications
Studying Modern Drama (2nd edn)
Studying Physics
Studying Programming
Studying Psychology
Teaching Study Skills and Supporting
  Learning
Work Placements – A Survival Guide for
  Students
Write it Right
Writing for Engineers (3rd edn)

Palgrave Study Guides: Literature

General Editors: John Peck and Martin Coyle
How to Begin Studying English Literature
  (3rd edn)
How to Study a Jane Austen Novel (2nd edn)
How to Study a Charles Dickens Novel
How to Study Chaucer (2nd edn)
How to Study an E. M. Forster Novel
How to Study James Joyce
How to Study Linguistics (2nd edn)

How to Study Modern Poetry
How to Study a Novel (2nd edn)
How to Study a Poet (2nd edn)
How to Study a Renaissance Play
How to Study Romantic Poetry (2nd edn)
How to Study a Shakespeare Play (2nd edn)
How to Study Television
Practical Criticism

Other books by Alan Clarke

e-Learning Skills (Palgrave Macmillan, 2004)
New CLAIT Level 1 Student Workbook
  (Hodder and Stoughton, 2002)

CLAIT Plus Level 2 Student Workbook
  (Hodder and Stoughton, 2003)

IT Skills for Successful Study

Alan Clarke

First published 2005 by
PALGRAVE MACMILLAN
Houndmills, Basingstoke, Hampshire RG21 6XS and
175 Fifth Avenue, New York, N.Y. 10010
Companies and representatives throughout the world

PALGRAVE MACMILLAN is the global academic imprint of the Palgrave
Macmillan division of St. Martin's Press, LLC and of Palgrave Macmillan Ltd.
Macmillan® is a registered trademark in the United States, United Kingdom
and other countries. Palgrave is a registered trademark in the European
Union and other countries.

ISBN 1–4039–9271–1

This book is printed on paper suitable for recycling and made from fully
managed and sustained forest sources.

A catalogue record for this book is available from the British Library.

10 9 8 7 6 5 4 3 2 1
14 13 12 11 10 09 08 07 06 05

Printed and bound in Great Britain by Antony Rowe Ltd, Chippenham, Wiltshire

Contents

Acknowledgements

I would like to thank my wife Christine for her continued help, support and tolerance in assisting the writing of this book.

The author and publishers wish to acknowledge Microsoft Corporation and NIACE for the use of their screen capture images.

Microsoft® product screen shots reprinted with permission from Microsoft Corporation.

Microsoft trademark acknowledged.

Introduction

While information and communication technology (ICT) can be a valuable aid to your studies, it does depend to some extent on your skills and understanding. It is likely that you have already used computer applications and e-mail in other contexts, perhaps during your school experience or at work. This book assumes that readers already have basic ICT skills, and is based around intermediate-level skills and knowledge, with some advanced-level content. The emphasis is on using ICT for studying (for example, helping you to write longer documents with footnotes, analysis of numerical data and presentation of findings). Each chapter is divided into sections to maximize your choice of what to study. The use of ICT in education differs from that of technology in employment or leisure. For example you will most probably need to:

- write longer documents integrating tables, images and data from other applications
- analyse data from experiments and projects
- present numerical data as charts and graphs
- make presentations based on the results of investigations
- engage in online communication: e-mail is now a major way of communicating with tutors, other students and college resources (such as the library)
- locate information (for example on the World Wide Web)
- have a general understanding of a computer system to organize your files efficiently.

Activities and examples to help you gain the most from the book are provided.

The chapters in the book can be summarized as:

Introduction
This introduction outlines what is involved with studying at university, and how information and communication technology can help you to be successful.

Chapter 1: Writing (Microsoft® Word)
This chapter assumes you have used Word to produce straightforward documents, and builds on this experience so that you can exploit Word to produce longer and better presented documents.

Chapter 2: Working with numbers (Microsoft® Excel)
This chapter assumes you have some experience of entering text and numbers into applications, and extends this experience so that you can mathematically model and analyse information. In addition it helps you present numerical information in the form of charts and graphs.

Chapter 3: Communication (Microsoft Outlook®)
This chapter assumes some experience in sending and receiving e-mail, and offers the opportunity to use an e-mail management application to organize yourself and your studies.

Chapter 4: Finding information (Microsoft® Internet Explorer)
This chapter assumes that you have begun to explore the World Wide Web, and provides you with help to improve your searching and judgement of online information.

Chapter 5: Organizing information (Microsoft® Access)
This chapter assumes that you have little experience of creating databases, and assists you to learn how to exploit a database as part of your learning.

Chapter 6: Presenting (Microsoft PowerPoint®)
This chapter assumes you have little experience of presenting or using visual aids, and provides you with the opportunity to develop a presentation.

Chapter 7: Managing your system (Microsoft Windows®)
This chapter assumes only limited experience of operating systems, and helps you to organize yourself.

▶ Overview

Studying at university requires that you take responsibility for your own learning, and for many new students, this is a significant challenge. It is your responsibility to plan your studies so that you are able to attend lectures, seminars, laboratories and other learning activities. You will have to record information so that it will help you understand the topics, and assist you when you need to revise for later examinations. Submission of your assignments and other forms of assessment in accordance with the college standards is essential. This all requires that you manage your time effectively, organize yourself so that you meet deadlines, consider future needs (such as revising for examinations), and communicate capably with fellow students, your teachers and college administrators. This has always been important, but as you are likely nowadays to be combining your studies with part-time employment, managing yourself is now critical.

To study at university you will need to be capable of undertaking a variety of activities such as:

- writing essays and other assignments
- analysing information
- communicating effectively with peers and tutors
- presenting information
- researching your subject
- organizing information
- learning independently.

Your written work is one of the main ways on which your tutors will base their judgement of you. If you provide high-quality written assignments, you will gain the credit that they deserve. Even if you completely understand the subject, if you are unable to provide a reasoned, well-presented written argument, you will gain little recognition for your work. Academic work requires that you follow accepted conventions which other environments do not. You are expected to use published work to support your reasoning and conclusions. It is vital that these are referenced to acknowledge the source.

In almost all courses you will be required to analyse information, both numerical and qualitative. You need to show that you can evaluate and investigate data in all forms to reach conclusions. These may be the results of practical work that you have undertaken or information obtained through reviewing literature. Analysis can involve mathematical processes, visual comparison of data, or structured presentation. In all cases information technology can assist you by means of applications such as spreadsheets, tables, charts and graphs.

Communication is a central element in all forms of education. In a large college with thousands of students, you are likely to find that a large amount of information will be provided online. Many courses will provide timetables, details of administrative arrangements and even the results of assignments on their department networks or virtual learning environments (VLEs). Your fellow students are likely to live complex, busy lives, combining part-time jobs with their studies, so that communication with them may be difficult. Group learning activities will be correspondingly demanding to coordinate. Your tutors have many calls on their time, so speaking to them may also require persistence. Communication technology can help you overcome or reduce many of these problems.

Many courses now require you to make presentations to your tutors and peers. This involves integration of investigations of a topic to identify what you need to present, consideration of how to put forward the key points, and communication with your audience. An added dimension is that the presentation is likely to be assessed and time-limited. Presentation applications (such as Microsoft PowerPoint®) offer a means of organizing yourself to provide a professional talk.

Research is a fundamental part of all education, involving a range of processes and activities including searching for relevant information, assessing its importance, suitability and reliability, as well as recording your conclusions, organizing the information and ensuring you can locate the source again. The Internet is now a major source of information on virtually all subjects. College libraries have also used technology not only to catalogue their collections but also to provide access to it. All this makes having the skills to use online resources and technology essential.

A key element in any investigation is organization of the information and sources that are found. There are numerous ways of doing this, including traditional ones such as files and papers, but databases are useful in that they have the additional advantages of allowing you to compare and contrast, adjust presentation and print out contents.

Managing your studies is your responsibility. You need to organize your time so that you meet your deadlines, allow time for the preparation of assignments, make available opportunities to reflect on your learning, and live a healthy life. This is not easy, especially if you are also working part-time and need to integrate the demands of studying and work. Computer applications will assist you to plan your time, and help remind you of time limits, objectives and critical goals. They cannot give you extra time, but they can help you make the most of what you have.

ICT can help you study successfully. Most colleges provide extensive access to computers and networks, with the expectation that students will employ these resources. VLEs are widely used to provide students with access to many learning and administrative resources. Tutors will frequently provide notes, handouts and references in electronic format.

1 Writing (Microsoft® Word)

▶ Overview

A key focus of the university experience is writing. Your successes will often be dependent on the quality of your written work, in that assignments are often the main way that you are judged. A few spelling mistakes may undermine the value of your work, since they give the appearance of carelessness. Nevertheless, a wonderful presentation will not overcome a lack of understanding and reasoning.

Writing is not always formal, and informal writing is still a vital part of learning. Your ability to take notes in lectures, from books and other sources is central to the learning experience. These represent key resources which you will need to use during revision many months later, so clarity and quality are important. Tutors will also provide handouts, notes and reading lists, and increasingly these documents are provided in electronic form. Many lecturers will place their lecture notes on the college intranet, virtual learning environment or other online source. This provides the opportunity to enhance these handouts through electronic annotation and store them for future use.

Learning is not simply an individual experience. Many assignments will require you to work as part of a group. This will often involve you in collaborative writing, where each member of the group is allocated an agreed task and these need to be brought together to form the finished result.

Information and communication technology can help you to produce high-quality written documents for all these purposes.

▶ Introduction

Word processing is probably the mostly widely used of computer applications, and you are likely to have some existing skills, so this chapter will concentrate on helping you to develop additional ones. The emphasis will be on developing skills relevant to studying, such as:

- writing essays
- tracking changes for collaborative work
- producing long documents (such as dissertations)
- improving the appearance of assignments.

To produce an essay or any form of written assignment takes a great deal of effort, and your marks will be based on the work that you submit. The presentation of your work is therefore essential. Your effort will not be fully rewarded if you do not present a high-quality document that does justice to your hard work. Word processing offers a variety of ways to present your work effectively.

The chapter covers:

- how word processing can help your writing
- large documents
- headers and footers
- tables (manipulating rows and columns; editing layout)
- borders
- bullets
- footnotes and endnotes
- page layout
- inserting images
- indexing/table of contents
- managing/editing documents (spellchecker/thesaurus, word counts and so on)
- merging and combining documents from different applications
- annotating e-documents
- printing.

The chapter is based on Microsoft® Word, which is available in several versions:

- Word 95
- Word 97
- Word 2000
- Word 2002.

You may be using any of these, since they represent the development of the product over the past nine years. People often purchase Microsoft® Office, which is a range of integrated products (word processing, spreadsheets, databases and so on). Microsoft® Office is again available in a range of versions (such as Office 95, Office 97, Office 2000 and Office XP) that align with the version of the individual products. Microsoft® Office XP combines applications which are individually designated as Word 2002, Excel 2002 and so on. The techniques described in this chapter will be based on Word 2002. However, you will be able to transfer them to any version of Word to which you have access, and hints and tips are given to make this easier.

In all versions of Microsoft® Office applications there are keyboard shortcuts. These allow you to select a function by pressing different combinations of keys rather than using menus and options. Keyboard shortcuts are shown by an underlined letter in the menu or option (for example Table tells you that to open the Table menu in Word you press the Alt key together with the 'a' key). There are many different shortcuts, and a full list can be obtained using the application Help function.

▶ Ways that word processing can help your writing

There are many ways that word processing can help your writing, and Table 1.1 lists 14 of them. Few people can write a good essay, assignment, report or dissertation at a first attempt. Well-written documents are the product of careful and systematic editing. The word processor allows you to check and amend your written work easily without losing what you have already produced. You can start with a brief outline of the areas you intend to cover and then build your assignment on the framework. Word processing allows you unlimited opportunities to edit your words to improve the content and presentation.

▶ Large documents

One of the main differences you will discover when producing pieces of writing as part of your course is that they are likely to be longer that you normally would produce. It is rare in life to write 1000 or 3000 words unless requested to do so. During a course you will often be asked as

Table 1.1 Improve your writing

Word processing technique	Benefit
1 Header and footer	Improve appearance and makes your documents professional
2 Page numbers	Make it easy to locate and read information
3 Borders	Improve presentation
4 Bullets	Break information into a meaningful list which will help readability and understanding
5 Footnotes	Allow you to add extra details to your documents
6 References	Let you to create references in the text linked to a list at the end of the document
7 Page layouts	Improve appearance and readability of document
8 Tables	Allow you to present complex information in a systematic and logical way.
9 Inserting images	A picture is often worth many additional words and will help understanding
10 Spell checking	Removes the small errors that will often distract readers from the value of your work
11 Thesaurus	Provides you with the means to extend your vocabulary and improve readability
12 Tracking changes	You can identify changes that you or a colleague have made to your document
13 Integrating information	Allows you to integrate different types of information from different applications (numbers, words, charts etc) to form a coherent document
14 Sub-headings	Provide a structure that will help readability and understanding

part of an assignment to write an essay of a certain length, and occasionally you will be told a maximum length, which is equally daunting. Word processing can help with your writing, since it allows you to:

- continuously check the length of your work
- edit your work to add or remove content to meet your target
- change the structure (adding and removing headings and sub-headings)
- check the spelling and grammar of your work to improve its quality
- check the language of your work with the thesaurus so that you can vary the words.

The word length will rarely impose a structure, the use of pictures or other forms of illustration on you. However, your college may have style guides or norms that limit or prevent your use of pictures. Word processing allows you to add:

- pictures
- figures
- tables
- indexes
- content lists.

These can add considerable value to your essays or other forms of assignment.

Word processing allows you to make significant changes to your written documents without having to start again, but actually it helps to spend a little time considering what you are aiming to produce. You need to plan your documents, at least in outline, to ensure that you achieve the best results. When you are developing the answer to an assignment, you are given a clear statement of what your examiner wants you to achieve. This provides you with a structure, so consider the assignment for guidance. Many examiners say that students fail to read the guidance they provide, so read it carefully and ask questions if you are not sure of anything.

▶ Headers and footers

Figure 1.1 shows a simple example of the use of a header and footer. In this case the header indicates the title of the paper and the author on each page, while in the footer the pages are numbered and the document dated. Once you have created a header and footer, the information will appear on every page. You can create complex or simple headers and footers depending on what you wish to achieve. A requirement of many assignments is that on every page you provide your name. Headers and footers offer you the means of ensuring that you comply with this condition.

The header and footer are located within the top and bottom margins of the page. When you move to a new page the header and footer information, which is greyed out, will appear automatically.

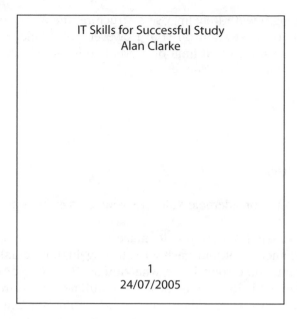

Figure 1.1 Header and footer

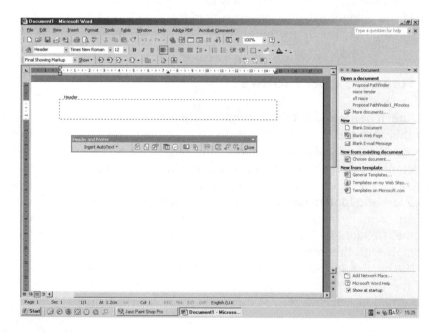

Figure 1.2 Header and Footer options onscreen

To create a header and footer:

1. Click on the View menu and select the Header and Footer option. (This is correct in many versions of Microsoft® Word, including Word 97 and Word 2002, although earlier versions of Word are very similar.) This opens the function, and Figure 1.2 shows what appears in Word 2002. The area in which the header and footer appears is indicated by a dotted rectangle.
2. Click into this area, insert text using the keyboard, and format it using the normal word processing functions of align left, centre, align right or justify. The Header and Footer toolbar offers several standard functions such as:

Activity   Header and footer

Start a new document and click on the View menu then select the Header and Footer option. Create a header which inserts the paper's title and the author of the document. Create a footer which numbers each page and gives the date that the document was created. If you are currently writing an essay or another type of assignment, add a header and footer to it.

Explore using the autotext options as well as entering the text from the keyboard. If you cannot see the header or footer on your page you will need to click on the Print Layout option in the View menu. In earlier versions of Word (such as Word 97), the option is called Page Layout.

Feedback
One approach is shown in Figure 1.3. This is a header and footer produced using the autotext option of Author, Page #, Date and then entering the text manually.

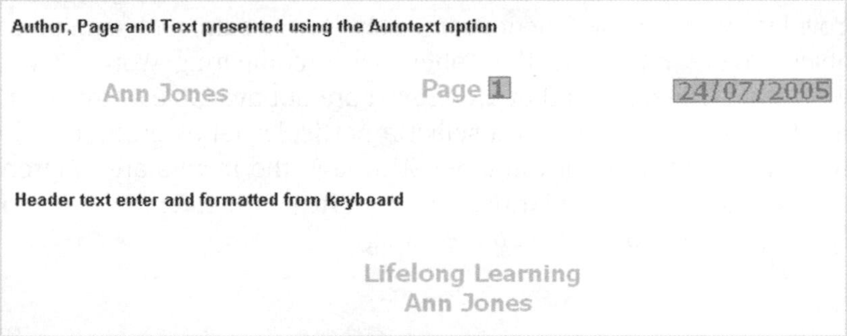

Author, Page and Text presented using the Autotext option

Ann Jones   Page 1   24/07/2005

Header text enter and formatted from keyboard

Lifelong Learning
Ann Jones

Figure 1.3 Header and footer activity

- Insert Page Number
- Insert Number of Pages
- Format Page Number
- Date
- Time
- Page Setup
- Show Hide.

▶ Tables

Tables enable you to present complex information so that it can be compared and contrasted. This is very useful in that it will often save you long explanations needed to achieve the same purpose in a narrative. However, if your table is too complex (with many rows and columns), you could instead confuse your readers. An effective table relates to the needs of readers, integrates with the text and serves an appropriate purpose.

Tables should be introduced in the text, with a clear link made between them and the rest of the document. It is generally good practice to locate a table close to the text that relates to it. A few moments spent considering what you want to achieve with your table is a good investment. There are significant differences between presenting the results of an engineering experiment and analysing Shakespeare plays. You need to consider the information, your purpose and who your readers are. In all assignments you are seeking to demonstrate your understanding of the subject, objectivity and analytical skills.

Many versions of Microsoft® Word have a menu called Table, which provides a variety of functions to help you create and manipulate tables. Figure 1.4 shows the Table menu, comparing Word 97 with Word 2002. The options that are greyed are not available at this point: they become active when you select a particular table, group of cells, rows or other feature of the table. Although the menus are different, there are still many similarities that will help you to create tables in whatever version of Word you are using.

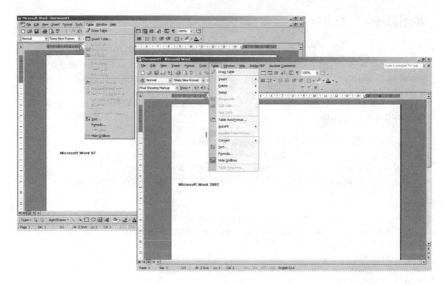

Figure 1.4 Table menu

To create a table:

1. Select the T_a_ble menu and highlight the _I_nsert option to reveal a sub-menu.
2. Click on the _T_able option to reveal the Insert Table window.
3. Create a table with specific numbers of rows and columns using the Insert Table window options.

The T_a_ble menu provides you with a range of functions to help you change the format and layout of your table. Some of the options are:

- Draw table: opens a toolbox of functions.
- Insert: add extra rows and columns.
- Delete: remove table, row, column or cell.
- Select: highlight table, row, column or cell.
- Merge cells: join two highlighted cells.
- Split cell: separate a highlighted cell into two.
- Autofit: fit contents into table.
- Convert: change text into a table or a table into text.

Activity Table

Create a table to compare and contrast the information from a survey of traffic at a road junction to assess the impact on the environment. The survey measured the number of passenger cars containing one or more passengers and those with only the driver, light commercial vehicles and heavy goods vehicles passing through the junction each hour. It counted the number of vehicles over a four-hour period covering the rush hour.

7 to 8 am: 15 cars, 4 cars with passengers, 2 light and 3 heavy goods vehicles.
8 to 9 am: 22 cars, 8 cars with passengers, 12 light and 9 heavy goods vehicles.
9 to 10 am: 12 cars, 3 cars with passengers, 16 light and 11 heavy goods vehicles
10 to 11 am: 9 cars, 2 cars with passengers, 19 light and 12 heavy goods vehicles.

Feedback
Figure 1.5 is an example of a table that provides this information. This was created by clicking on the Table menu, highlighting the Insert option to reveal a menu and then selecting the Table option to open the Insert Table window. The number of rows and columns was chosen by clicking on the arrow buttons alongside the Number of columns and Number of rows lines. The number is shown in the corresponding box.

Time	Cars	Cars with passengers	Light commercial vehicles	Heavy goods vehicles
7 to 8 am	15	4	2	3
8 to 9 am	22	8	12	9
9 to 10 am	12	3	16	11
10 to 11 am	9	2	19	12

Figure 1.5 Survey table

In this sample all rows and columns are equal in size, and the information is left aligned. Word contains a variety of tools to help you manipulate the appearance and layout. The next activity provides you with the opportunity to practise changing the layout and format of tables.

The normal procedure is to select (highlight) the item you want to manipulate and then carry out the change. In addition to the Table menu you can also employ the normal alignment (for example, centre) and format options (such as bold, font and character size) available within Word on the formatting toolbar. Again, you need to highlight the cell or cells you want to change and then select the new format or alignment.

It is also possible to change the size of the table using the mouse:

1. Position the mouse pointer near to the column or row line and you will see it change shape (Figure 1.6).
2. Hold down the mouse button.
3. Drag the row or column line to change its size.

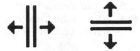

Figure 1.6 Shape of pointer

Activity   Manipulating a table

Using the table you created in the previous activity, experiment with improving the appearance of the table using the standard alignment and format functions within Word and in the Table menu.

Feedback
Figure 1.7 shows how the appearance and format of the table have been improved by:

- Centring the titles of each column by highlighting them and selecting the centre option on the formatting toolbar.
- Emboldening the titles by highlighting and selecting the bold option on the formatting toolbar.
- Centring the data but leaving the row titles left aligned by highlighting them and selecting the centre option on the formatting toolbar.

Time	Cars		Commercial vehicles	
	Cars	Cars with passengers	Light commercial vehicles	Heavy goods vehicles
7 to 8 am	15	4	2	3
8 to 9 am	22	8	12	9
9 to 10 am	12	3	16	11
10 to 11 am	9	2	19	12

Figure 1.7 Revised table

Activity   Manipulating a table – *continued*

- Emboldening the row titles by selecting them and choosing the bold option.
- Placing the mouse pointer in top row and selecting the Table menu, highlighting the Insert option to reveal the menu, then clicking on the Insert Rows Above option. A new blank row is added to the table. Select (highlight) the two cells above 'Cars' and 'Cars with passengers', then select Table menu and Merge Cells. The chosen cells merge to form a single cell. Repeat this action for the two cells above 'Light commercial vehicles' and 'Heavy goods vehicles'. Select the blank cell above the 'Time' title and the 'Time' title cell itself, and again merge them. Add the titles 'Cars' and 'Commercial vehicles', centring and emboldening them.
- Positioning the mouse on the column and row lines to change the size of the columns to better fit the contents of the 'Time' column.

How did your experiment work out?

▶ Borders

The appearance of any document is important. The document will initially be judged on the professional image it presents. Borders are a means of improving the look and feel of your work. However, they have other important roles such as drawing readers' attention to examples, quotes or case studies. They illustrate that the enclosed content is important. If you are presenting a series of examples through your report, the use of the same border will indicate to your readers that these are the same sort of example. Borders are probably best employed selectively. If over-used, borders will probably distract and confuse.

Microsoft® Word provides you with a range of options related to creating borders around pages, tables and other boxes within documents. It enables you to highlight examples or case studies within your paper. The secret of employing borders as an attention-drawing device is to use them sparingly and consistently, so that your readers do not become complacent about their use. A decorative border may well become a negative factor if over-used. To access the borders option:

1. Select the Format menu.
2. Choose the Borders and Shading option to reveal the Borders and Shading window (Figure 1.8).

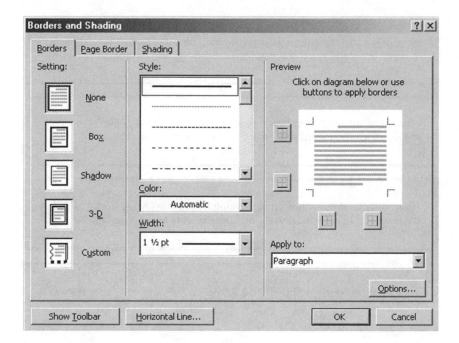

Figure 1.8 Borders and Shading menu

This process is the same in a range of versions of Word (such as Word 97 and Word 2002). Alternatively you can use the Tables and Borders function on the standard toolbar, or if you are creating a table, you can access the Borders and Shading window through the Table Properties option in Word 2002. In all Microsoft® Office applications you will find that there are many alternative ways of carrying out a function.

The Borders and Shading window (Figure 1.8) allows you to choose between a variety of options such as:

- borders or shading
- widths of line
- colour of line
- styles of line (such as dotted).

You can create a border around either a single paragraph (or series of paragraphs) or the whole page. The whole page functions are available within the Page Border tab. Figure 1.9 gives some examples of the different types of border that you can create.

Information and communication technology provides many useful tools for students including word processing, spreadsheets and databases

Information and communication technology provides many useful tools for students including word processing, spreadsheets and databases

Information and communication technology provides many useful tools for students including word processing, spreadsheets and databases

Information and communication technology provides many useful tools for students including word processing, spreadsheets and databases

Figure 1.9 Examples of borders and shading

Activity   Borders

Experiment with changing the border of the table you created in the previous activities. Try to make the border line thicker.

Feedback
Figure 1.10 shows the outcomes of a series of changes:

1. The first table has been changed to have thicker borders. This was achieved by placing the mouse pointer within the table and highlighting it using the Select option within the Table menu. The Borders and Shading window provides the option to change the line thickness.
2. The second example has been changed to have a thicker outside border line with the original thickness internal or grid lines. This was achieved by highlighting the table and using the Grid option of the border styles.
3. The third example has been changed to have a treble outside border line with the original thickness internal or grid lines. This was achieved by highlighting the table and using the Style options.

What did you manage to create?

Activity   Borders – *continued*

Time	Cars		Commercial vehicles	
	Cars	Cars with passengers	Light commercial vehicles	Heavy goods vehicles
7 to 8 am	15	4	2	3
8 to 9 am	22	8	12	9
9 to 10 am	12	3	16	11
10 to 11 am	9	2	19	12

Time	Cars		Commercial vehicles	
	Cars	Cars with passengers	Light commercial vehicles	Heavy goods vehicles
7 to 8 am	15	4	2	3
8 to 9 am	22	8	12	9
9 to 10 am	12	3	16	11
10 to 11 am	9	2	19	12

Time	Cars		Commercial vehicles	
	Cars	Cars with passengers	Light commercial vehicles	Heavy goods vehicles
7 to 8 am	15	4	2	3
8 to 9 am	22	8	12	9
9 to 10 am	12	3	16	11
10 to 11 am	9	2	19	12

Figure 1.10 Revised table

▶ Bullets

A key objective in all forms of writing is to produce an easy to read and understandable document. One way to improve readability is to present information in the form of a list. Word lets you use a series of bullets or a numbered list. These are accessed by selecting the Format menu and the Bullets and Numbering option to open the Bullets and Numbering window. This is almost an identical process in many versions of Word. It provides you with several choices of bullets, ways of numbering and opportunities to customize them.

If you select a bullet type by single-clicking on a style, you will see the Customize button become active. If you click this button you will reveal the customize bullet list window, which allows you to customize your bullets. Within this window is the Picture button, which provides access to many picture bullets. You should explore the options.

The Customize Bullet List window allows you to select fonts, to pick bullets from many different characters, and to use pictures as bullets. The window also lets you change the position of the bullets and preview them. When you have made your choices you need to click the OK button to apply them to your document.

Although lists help readability, it is good practice to limit their use. They are a useful device when you want to present a large amount of information in a systematic way. It is effective practice to use bullets or lists in a consistent way throughout a document. This presents a professional approach and avoids distracting your reader through a range of approaches.

The use of bullets and lists is not always appropriate. In some courses and subjects your tutor is likely to discourage their use. It is therefore sensible to check with your tutor, or consider style guides or other forms of advice provided by your college or department before using them.

▶ Footnotes

Footnotes often form part of academic papers. They are extra remarks relating to a comment in the main body of text that the author prefers to position outside the main document. The link is shown by providing a footnote number in the main body text and linking it to a numbered footnote. Footnotes, normally placed at the bottom of the page, can be a useful method of adding explanation, but like many other devices they should not be overused since they can sometimes be a distraction for readers. To add a footnote using Word:

1. Highlight the item in the main text that you want to link to the footnote.
2. Select the Insert menu and highlight the Reference option to open an extra menu of four choices:
   - Footnote
   - Caption
   - Cross-reference
   - Index and Tables.
3. Click on the Footnote option to open the Footnote and Endnote window. You can then make changes to the position of the note and how it is numbered. In earlier versions of Word (such as Word 97) the option is called Footnote, and this directly opens the Footnote and Endnote window, which contains fewer options.

Figure 1.11 shows an example of a footnote. The numbered item in the text and the footnote have been highlighted inside a box and arrowed so that you can see them. Obviously in the actual document the boxes and arrows are not shown.

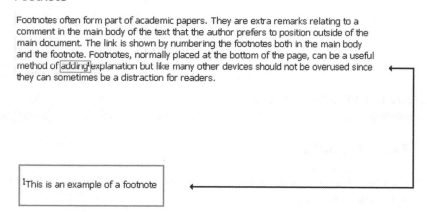

Footnote

Footnotes often form part of academic papers. They are extra remarks relating to a comment in the main body of the text that the author prefers to position outside of the main document. The link is shown by numbering the footnotes both in the main body and the footnote. Footnotes, normally placed at the bottom of the page, can be a useful method of adding explanation but like many other devices should not be overused since they can sometimes be a distraction for readers.

[1]This is an example of a footnote

Figure 1.11 Footnote

Endnotes are very similar to footnotes except that the note is placed at the end of the document. Each note is numbered in the text and then in the list at the end of the document, making a list of references linked to numbered items in the text. However, there are other ways of showing references, and you need to find out the style required for your document. Journals and colleges often have their own standards for references. Figure 1.12 illustrates how endnotes work.

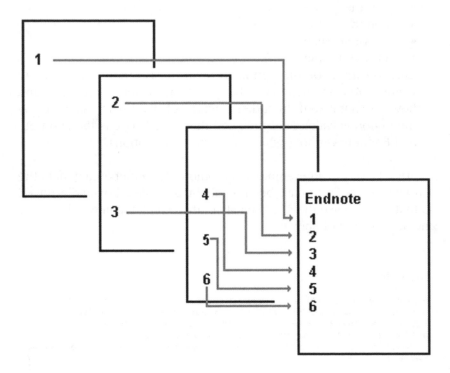

Figure 1.12 Endnote for references

▶ Page layouts

The layout of a page is determined by a combination of many different factors. These include:

- page margins
- orientation
- line spacing
- alignment of text
- paragraph indents
- line and page breaks
- columns.

Margins

With Word you can vary all four margins (top, bottom, left and right). This is often combined with the orientation of the paper (portrait or landscape). Figure 1.13 illustrates the different margins and orientation. You will sometimes be asked to provide large left or right margins in order to allow feedback to be added to your assignments. Some tutors will also ask you to provide your work double spaced, to again allow sufficient space for comments.

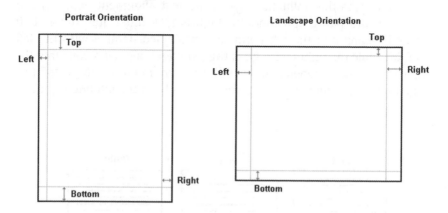

Figure 1.13 Margins and orientation

To set the margins:

1. Select the File menu.
2. Select the Page Setup option to open the Page Setup window.

This is also the approach in earlier versions of Word. The page setup window allows you to set margins by using the up and down arrow buttons, while orientation is established by clicking on the portrait or landscape option in the middle of the window. There is also an option to set the size of the gutter, which is additional space to allow you to bind the pages without losing any of the text when the page is folded. You can set a gutter to the left or top of the page depending on how you are binding the document. There is also a facility to preview the layout changes at the bottom of the window.

Line spacing, alignment and paragraphs

You are frequently asked to produce assignments, dissertations or theses with double or other line spacings. This is to allow the marker to add comments to your work to help you understand weaknesses or misunderstandings. However, readability is often helped by providing more white (empty) space on the page, so increasing the line spacing can be helpful even when this is not a specific requirement. A common error is to select a small font size when you are asked to write an assignment with a limited number of pages. It might allow you to write more, but only at the expense of readability. White space is often helpful.

Other factors that influence layout are text alignment (left, right or justified) and paragraph indents. Figure 1.14 illustrates these. Left aligned means that the left-hand text is aligned parallel with the left margin, while the right text edge is ragged. Right aligned means that the right-hand text is aligned parallel with the right margin with the left text edge ragged. Justified alignment means that both the left and right text

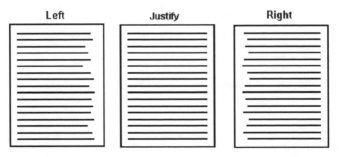

No indent

This is a paragraph without any indent. This is a paragraph without any indent. This is a paragraph without any indent. This is a paragraph without any indent. This is a paragraph without any indent. This is a paragraph without any indent. This is a paragraph without any indent. This is a paragraph without any indent.

Indent

This is a paragraph with an indent. This is a paragraph with an indent. This is a paragraph with an indent. This is a paragraph with an indent. This is a paragraph with an indent. This is a paragraph with an indent. This is a paragraph with an indent. This is a paragraph with an indent. This is a paragraph with an

Figure 1.14 Alignment and paragraph indents

edges are parallel with the left and right margins. 'Justify' is a Word term: this is sometimes called 'double justified' or 'fully justified' in other sources. There is also a fourth option called centred, in which the text is aligned with the centre of the page and both margins are ragged. This is often employed for titles or to gain the reader's attention.

Line spacing, alignment and paragraph indents are all accessed by selecting the Format menu and the Paragraph option to open the Paragraph window. These controls are designed to operate on a highlighted paragraph or other area of text.

In the Paragraph window there are two tabbed screens. The Indents and Spacing tab allows you to set the alignment of text, indentation and line spacing. You can also vary of the spacing before or after a paragraph (using the spacing before and after boxes). You can preview the changes in the area at the bottom of the window.

Line and page breaks

The Paragraph window has a second tabbed screen called Line and Page Break. This has controls for pagination, widows and orphans, and hyphenation.

- Pagination is the control of where a page break will happen. This is important to prevent related information being split across two pages. Word automatically inserts page breaks, but this control allows you to prevent paragraphs being split.
- Widows and orphans are the terms for a single line of text at the top or bottom of a page. This makes your document appear unprofessional, so Word provides the means of eliminating them.
- Hyphenation controls the point (if any) at which a word can be split onto two lines using a hyphen.

The Paragraph window Line and Page Break tab provides the following controls:

- widows and orphans (prevents them by changing the point at which the page ends)
- keep with next (keeps a paragraph on the same page as the next one)
- keep lines together (stops paragraphs being split over two pages)
- page break before (places a paragraph on the next page)
- don't hyphenate (stops automatic hyphenation in the chosen paragraph).

Automatic hyphenation is available by selecting the Tools menu, highlighting Language and choosing the Hyphenation option.

There is also a preview area and a Tabs button which opens the Tab window to enable you to set the spacing of tabs.

Activity   Layout practice

Enter the text below into Word.

Gettysburg is a small town in rural Pennsylvania about 30 miles from Harrisburg, the state capital. It was the site of one of the most famous battles in the history of the USA. The Confederate army of North Virginia commanded by General Robert E. Lee tried for three days to defeat the Union army. It failed and probably signalled the end of the Civil War although it took a further 18 months for the south to admit defeat.

Using the text:

1. Explore setting different margins (top, bottom, left and right).
2. Change the alignment to left, justified and right.
3. Indent the paragraph. Explore the first line, hanging and none settings in the special box, and view the changes in the preview area.
4. Change the display to two columns.

Feedback
Some examples are shown below.

First, this is the effect of setting large left and right margins.

> Gettysburg is a small town in rural Pennsylvania about 30 miles from Harrisburg, the state capital. It was the site of one of the most famous battles in the history of the USA. The Confederate army of North Virginia commanded by General Robert E. Lee tried for three days to defeat the Union army. It failed and probably signalled the end of the Civil War although it took a further 18 months for the south to admit defeat.

Here is the text left aligned:

Gettysburg is a small town in rural Pennsylvania about 30 miles from Harrisburg, the state capital. It was the site of one of the most famous battles in the history of the USA. The Confederate army of North Virginia commanded by General Robert E. Lee tried for three days to defeat the Union army. It failed and probably signalled the end of the Civil War although it took a further 18 months for the south to admit defeat.

Activity   Layout practice – *continued*

Now it is centre aligned:

Gettysburg is a small town in rural Pennsylvania about 30 miles from Harrisburg,
the state capital. It was the site of one of the most famous battles in the history of
the USA. The Confederate army of North Virginia commanded by General Robert E.
Lee tried for three days to defeat the Union army. It failed and probably signalled
the end of the Civil War although it took a further 18 months for the south to
admit defeat.

And now right aligned:

Gettysburg is a small town in rural Pennsylvania about 30 miles from Harrisburg,
the state capital. It was the site of one of the most famous battles in the history
of the USA. The Confederate army of North Virginia commanded by General Robert
E. Lee tried for three days to defeat the Union army. It failed and probably signalled
the end of the Civil War although it took a further 18 months for the south to
admit defeat.

This version has a hanging indent:

Gettysburg is a small town in rural Pennsylvania about 30 miles from Harrisburg, the
state capital. It was the site of one of the most famous battles in the history
of the USA. The Confederate army of North Virginia commanded by General
Robert E. Lee tried for three days to defeat the Union army. It failed and
probably signalled the end of the Civil War although it took a further 18
months for the south to admit defeat.

This is the effect of a first line indent:

Gettysburg is a small town in rural Pennsylvania about 30 miles from
Harrisburg, the state capital. It was the site of one of the most famous battles in the
history of the USA. The Confederate army of North Virginia commanded by General
Robert E. Lee tried for three days to defeat the Union army. It failed and probably
signalled the end of the Civil War although it took a further 18 months for the south
to admit defeat.

This version selects 'No special effects':

Gettysburg is a small town in rural Pennsylvania about 30 miles from Harrisburg, the
state capital. It was the site of one of the most famous battles in the history of the
USA. The Confederate army of North Virginia commanded by General Robert E. Lee
tried for three days to defeat the Union army. It failed and probably signalled the
end of the Civil War although it took a further 18 months for the south to admit
defeat.

Activity   Layout practice – *continued*

Finally, here is the text displayed in two columns:

Gettysburg is a small town in rural Pennsylvania about 30 miles from Harrisburg, the state capital. It was the site of one of the most famous battles in the history of the USA. The Confederate army of North Virginia commanded by General Robert E. Lee tried for three days to defeat the Union army. It failed and probably signalled the end of the Civil War although it took a further 18 months for the south to admit defeat.

With short passages of text like this columns are often ineffective: it is better use them for substantial blocks of text.

Columns

You may often want to produce columns within your documents, and to do this:

1. Select the F_ormat menu.
2. Select the C_olumns option to reveal the Columns window.

You can have multiple columns, vary their sizes, and divide the text into columns either for the whole document or from a particular point. This feature is also provided in earlier versions of Word (such as Word 97).

Newspapers often use a columnar display since this makes the text easy to read and gives it a pleasant appearance. You may want to employ columns if you are preparing a student newsletter, poster or other types of publication.

▶ Inserting images

Illustrations are a vital part of many documents. They add interest and will gain the attention of your readers. An image will help you explain your argument, and demonstrate your own understanding of the subject. When you are writing an essay, report or paper for your course, you are aiming to demonstrate your understanding of the topic. Frequently you are limited to a maximum number of words. An illustration will often not count towards the word total, while contributing to the quality of your work. However, an illustration should be closely linked to the text so that it integrates with and supports your discussion.

The use of illustrations is not always appropriate. In some courses and subjects your tutor is likely to discourage their use. It is therefore sensible to check with your tutor, or consider style guides or other forms of advice provided by your college or department, before using them.

In order to add an image to your document you need to:

1. Select the Insert menu.
2. Highlight the Picture option to reveal eight further options which relate to inserting images. They are:
   - Clip Art: to add a ready-made standard image.
   - From File: to add an image you have stored on your computer system. The images can be imported or created using applications such as Windows® Paint.
   - From Scanner or Camera: to scan an image into your document or insert a photograph taken with a digital camera.
   - Organization chart: to create an organization chart within your document.
   - New Drawing: to create a drawing area called the canvas on which you can draw diagrams, insert images or add drawings.
   - Autoshapes: to insert a range of shapes (such as rectangles).
   - WordArt: to add interesting effects to the text (for example curving text).
   - Chart: to create a chart.

Word groups together the drawing functions in the draw toolbar in all versions of the application, although later versions offer more functions. In Word 2002, this facility enables you to add clip art, insert a picture, create charts, rotate images, change the colour of areas, lines and text, and add shadow or three-dimensional effects to objects. Within the draw toolbar and the Insert menu is the Text Box function, with which you can create a text area to highlight information. If you were writing a report of a series of interviews, you might place interviewee quotes in text boxes to highlight them and so draw your readers' attention to them. When you select the text box, it appears surrounded by the drawing area (the canvas). However, you can drag the text box to your chosen location even if it is off the canvas.

Within the Windows® operating system there is a series of applications called accessories, of which Windows® Paint is one. It is a straightforward painting and drawing application with which you can create drawings, manipulate images and produce diagrams. It is often useful to create images within Paint and then insert them using the From File option. To open Windows® Paint:

1. Highlight the Programs option in the Start menu.
2. Highlight the Accessories option.
3. Click on the Paint option.

Figure 1.15 illustrates the Windows® Paint application.

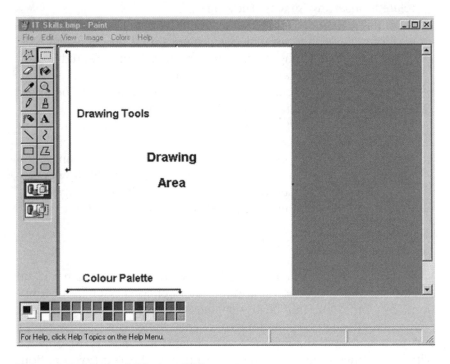

Figure 1.15 Microsoft Windows® Paint

Illustrations are an important part of many documents, but to employ them to the greatest effect you need to explain to your readers what they represent, and draw their attention to the key elements of the image. You should do this within the main body of the text. A caption for the image can also prove very useful, since this provides a cross-reference and additional explanation. Word provides the means to create captions and to number illustrations within your documents.

A common error in many documents is to give an illustration an incorrect number. Word's caption function helps reduce this type of mistake. To locate it:

1. Select the Insert menu.
2. Highlight the Reference option to reveal a sub-menu of options (Footnote, Caption, Cross-reference and Index and Tables).
3. Click on Caption to open the Caption window.

Activity   Autoshapes

Using the autoshapes, text box and colour fill features, create a diagram to represent the water cycle. This is the process in which water from the seas and oceans evaporates, condenses into clouds and then falls (precipitates) as rain. The rain then runs into the rivers and returns to the sea.

Feedback
Figure 1.16 is a simple effort using the standard shapes within AutoShape. The text was added using three text boxes, and colour was provided using the colour fill function.

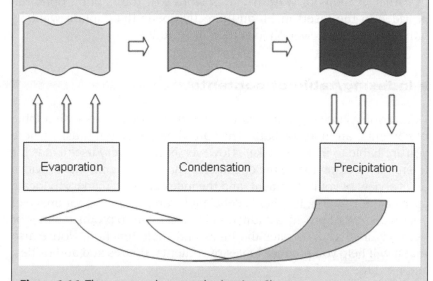

Figure 1.16 The water cycle, created using AutoShape

Activity   Autoshapes – *continued*

In Figure 1.17 Windows® Paint was used to create the same diagram. This kind of simple diagram requires no artistic talent, and you can probably improve upon it.

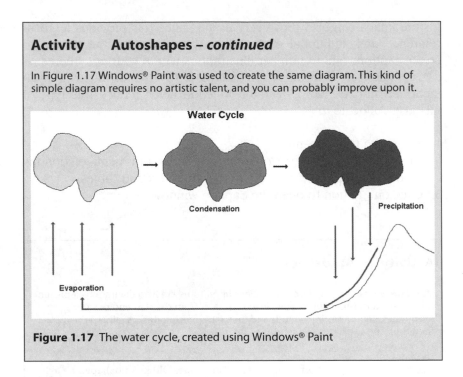

Figure 1.17 The water cycle, created using Windows® Paint

In earlier versions of Word (such as Word 97), the Caption option is provided in the Insert menu and directly opens the Caption window, although this has fewer options than in Word 2002.

▶ Indexing/table of contents

During your studies you may have to produce documents with a table of contents, an index or both. They are time-consuming tasks where you are liable to make mistakes. However, both are very useful aids for the reader seeking to use the document. The table of contents provides an overview of your document, and the index enables readers to locate specific information. If either is deficient it can present a poor image of your work. Word provides a function to assist you to produce either or both. Figure 1.18 illustrates the Index and Table function. Notice also that it will help you produce tables of contents, figures and authorities. You need to:

1. Select the Insert menu.

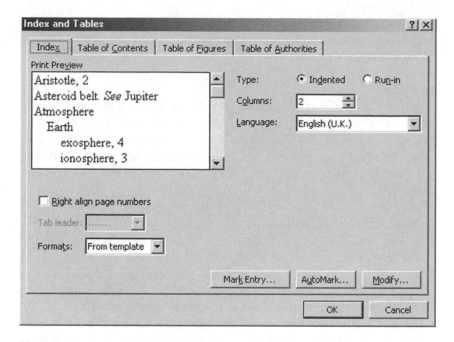

Figure 1.18 Index and tables

2. Highlight the Reference option to reveal additional options including Index and Tables.

In earlier versions of Word (such as Word 97), the Index and Tables option is provided in the Insert menu, and directly opens the Index and Tables window, although this has different options from those in Word 2002.

► Managing and editing documents

A major advantage of word processing is that you can edit your document to improve its quality. A range of functions to assist you in editing and managing your document are available in Word. They include:

- checking your spelling
- thesaurus
- tracking changes
- find and replace
- word count.

These are available in all versions of Word, although functions increase in the later versions. The greatest changes between versions are in the 'Track Changes' function.

Spelling

In any document it is important to remove spelling mistakes, since even a few will give the impression of a poor-quality effort. Word provides a spelling checker that will go through your document and locate words it feels are incorrect. It can also be set so that it identifies possible mistakes as you enter them. To access the spelling checker:

1. Select the Tools menu.
2. Select the Spelling and Grammar option. This will reveal the spelling and grammar window.
3. Notice that you can ask the function to check grammar as well as spelling, and that the spellchecker should be set to the English (UK) dictionary. A common mistake is to set the spellchecker to use a US English dictionary. This can lead to errors because of the differences between US and UK English (for example 'centre' in UK English is spelled 'center' in US English).

The Spelling and Grammar window provides an Options button that offers a range of additional choices. These include:

- checking spelling as you enter text
- ignoring Internet and file names
- checking grammar as you enter text.

The Settings button lets you set the options for the grammar checker.

Thesaurus

A thesaurus can be a useful aid when writing. For many readers the over-use of certain words or phrases will suggest a poor-quality document or a lack of effort. A thesaurus can provide alternative words to extend your vocabulary. To access Word's thesaurus:

1. Select the Tools menu.
2. Highlight the Language choice to reveal a sub-menu including the option Thesaurus. In earlier versions of Word (such as Word 97), the Thesaurus function is located in the same place.

Again you can choose to base your thesaurus on a UK English, US English, or other dictionary. It is important to choose the correct one. To select the dictionary:

1. Select the Tools menu.
2. Highlight the Language choice to reveal a sub-menu including the option Set Language. This allows you to select the language dictionary.

Tracking changes

In many courses you will be required to work as part of team when undertaking a project, which may mean that you have to submit a team report to which all team members contribute. This can be quite difficult, since you all need to be able to give your ideas in such a way that they can be distinguished from each and agreed to before changes are made. Word provides an effective way of tracking changes so that writing partners can see what each has done in detail, and then agree or disagree.

In order to use the track changes function you need to turn on the option by clicking on Track Changes in the Tools menu (this is also available in earlier versions of Word). In Word 2002, a toolbox is opened allowing you to select what changes are shown and how. When you make any subsequent amendment it is identified as shown in Figure 1.19. On the screen inserted words are shown in colour, but they appear as grey here. Once you have decided which changes you accept or reject, position the mouse pointer over them and click the right button to open a menu of options (Figure 1.19).

Tracking changes is a very useful function even when you are writing on your own, as it provides a second chance to check your amendments. There will be many occasions when you regret changes that you have made and have no way of remembering the original, or you are faced with time-consuming rewriting from a paper copy. Tracking changes provides a quick and straightforward way of turning the clock back.

Find and replace

There are many occasions when you need to change a word or phrase throughout a long document. You may have used an incorrect technical term, misunderstood the meaning of a particular word, or simply feel a different expression is better than the one you used. You can obviously work through the document and make the changes

Figure 1.19 Track changes and accept or reject changes

from the keyboard. The danger is that you will miss one or more of the words or phrases you are seeking to alter, or introduce mistakes into the text. Word provides a function to locate all the words or phrases you wish to change and then replace them with your new option. This is called Find and Replace, and it is available from the Edit menu. It is provided in two different ways from this menu in the form of the Find and then the Replace options. The Find and Replace window has three tabs from which you select different options. The Find tab lets you locate specific words, phrases and parts of words, the Replace tab provides the additional feature of replacing them with new words or phrases, and Go To moves the cursor to a specific page or other part of the text.

There is also a More button in the window that opens up extra options such as matching the case of your Find words with those in the text, locating only whole words, and identifying words or phrases that sound like your Find words.

Activity   Track changes

Type this short piece of text then edit it in Word with the track changes option switched on (select Tools menu and Track Changes). This will allow you to see how the function works. Alternatively choose a piece of your own work that needs to be edited and try the same task. In either case it is also useful to use the spelling checker and thesaurus once you have completed your changes. This is always good practice whenever you create an electronic document.

Information and communication technologies have changed many aspects of the society in which we live. The initial impact was centred on the work place but effects have expanded and are still growing with transformations in communication, information, eduction and training underway. As this process accelerates, its long term impact is not entirely clear but for individuals to be included in this emerging technological society requires them to be competent users of ICT (Clarke and Englebright; Candy, 2003).

Feedback
Figure 1.20 shows some efforts to edit the paragraph as they appear with 'Track Changes' visible. Compare this with the examples shown on page 32, of a document that has been edited then reopened.

Information and communication technologies **(ICT)** have changed many aspects of the society in which we live. The initial impact was centred on the work place but effects have expanded and are still growing with transformations in communication, information, **leisure, entertainment,** education and training underway. As this process accelerates, its long term impact is not entirely clear but for individuals to be included in this emerging technological society requires them to be competent users of ICT (Clarke and Englebright, **2003**; Candy, 2003).

Figure 1.20 Example of tracked changes

Word count

Many assignments require that you write to a maximum length, or show the length of your work. Word provides a function which lets you to check your word length as you create your assignment. To activate this:

1. Select the Tools menu.
2. Select the Word Count option. This counts the number of pages, words, characters, paragraphs and lines.

Activity   Word count

Explore the word count function with a document you have written. Highlight one section and notice that the word count will be limited to this section.

Feedback
Trying this exercise using about three and half chapters of the manuscript of this book showed that it consisted of:

1. 121 pages.
2. 22,598 words.
3. 1,748 paragraphs.

Highlighting a paragraph showed it to comprise:

1. 1 page.
2. 150 words.
3. 1 paragraph.

This function also provides information about the number of characters and lines.

Merging documents

Copying and pasting

Documents created by Microsoft® Office applications can be combined to form an integrated publication. Earlier we considered how to insert images into a Word document, an example of merging two files together (a word processing file with a Paint image). If you have undertaken a project that involves the analysis of quantitative information, you may have produced a spreadsheet. When you are writing your report you could obviously transfer your numeric results manually to a Word table, but this takes time and there is always the risk that you will make a mistake. It is far easier to copy the spreadsheet into Word. The simplest process is to highlight the material you want to transfer and copy it using the Copy function, then position the cursor at the place you would like to insert it, and paste it into the document (using the Edit menu and Paste option).

Combining documents

You will often need to join different Word documents together to form a combined document. In order to merge two files together you need to:

1. Position the cursor at the location where you want to add the new document.
2. Select the Insert menu then the File option.
3. Open the Insert File window and locate your file, which might be stored on the computer's hard disc, or a floppy disk, message stick or other storage medium. The process is similar in earlier versions of Word (such as Word 97).

Converting tables into text
If you are importing a textual table into a document you will occasionally need to remove the table framework and convert the contents into text. The reverse is also required occasionally (that is, to convert text into a table). Word 2002 provides this function in the Table menu, within the option Convert, which is activated once you have highlighted the table or text. In some earlier versions of Word (such as Word 97) these functions are not available.

▶ Annotating e-documents

Many tutors provide handouts as an aid to understanding their presentations and practical work. These are often available during classes and in electronic form by downloading files from the college website, virtual learning environment or intranet. Learning is enhanced if you are able to annotate handouts. You can then record your own impressions against the standard text. In the classroom you will often write notes directly on the handout. This is a useful way of capturing your immediate thoughts and adding extra value.

When the handout is also provided in electronic form, you have the additional opportunity of writing up your rough notes directly on the handout. Your learning is likely to be enhanced if you revisit your notes, and rewriting them will help you later when you are revising, since word processed notes are likely to be clearer than rough notes taken during a lecture. Word processing allows you to add your extra notes in a different colour to distinguish between the original text and your annotation. Word also contains an electronic highlighter so that you can highlight significant points.

To change the text colour or to highlight text, select the appropriate icons on the formatting toolbar. Figure 1.21 shows the Word 2002 toolbar and identifies other useful tools. All versions of Word offer similar functions on the toolbar.

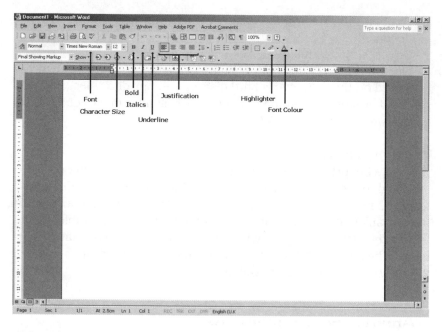

Figure 1.21 Formatting toolbar

Hyperlinks

It is possible to insert hyperlinks within a Word document, enabling you to link to a specific webpage, e-mail address or file. This is useful if you want to show relationships within your study notes to other resources, and provides a comprehensive document when you are revising, reviewing a topic or seeking information for an assignment. To insert a link:

1. Select the Insert menu.
2. Click on the Hyperlink option to open the Insert Hyperlink window.

This is also available in earlier versions of Word (such as Word 97), although with fewer options than in Word 2002.

Inserting comments

It is often useful to annotate a document (for example, to add extra notes to a handout). Word has a Comments feature through which you can include your own comments in a document. To add comments:

1. Position the cursor where you would like to link the comment to appear.
2. Select the Insert menu and the Comment option.
3. Enter your text in the Comments box.

Earlier versions of Word (such as Word 97) provide the same function. The comment can be amended by clicking on it and adding, changing or deleting the text.

There are many reasons for including comments, such as:

- adding extra content to standard handouts
- giving feedback to group members working on a joint assignment
- recording ideas as you work through your own notes
- making links to other work
- recording verbal feedback in the appropriate place
- reminding yourself of things you intend to change or develop.

Comments are especially useful if you are collaborating with other students on a joint project or other form of assignment. You can send your group your views on the written outcomes, cross-referenced to the exact place in the document. This is very helpful in avoiding confusion. Oral comments are easy to misunderstand, while written notes present you with problem of relating them to the exact point in the document. Comments combine clarity of written feedback with an exact cross-reference.

▶ Printing

Printing is a key part of word processing since in most cases you will want to produce a printed copy of any document you have created. Word has a number of functions to control the printing process. To access them:

1. Select the File menu.
2. Choose the Print option to open the Print window.

This menu also offers the option to check the appearance of your print-outs by selecting the File menu and Print Preview. It is good practice always to preview your documents, as it will avoid making mistakes and also save paper.

Top tips

1. **Editing:** The quality of any document relates to the number of times you are able to review its contents and add, subtract and amend the contents. Word processing allows you to edit your own words efficiently and effectively. Give yourself time to review your work and gain the benefit of editing.
2. **Managing:** Large documents need to be managed so that they are well presented and meet the needs of your course (for example with references, indexes and tracked changes).
3. **Checking:** A few spelling mistakes, overuse of certain words or exceeding the word limit can devalue your work. The few moments required to spell check your work, run the thesaurus and count the number of words in a document can help you considerably.
4. **Annotation:** Adding to standard handouts or your own notes can prove a useful aid to your learning and revision.

▶ Summary

1.   Header and footer: click on the View menu and select the Header and Footer option.
2.   To create a table, select the Table menu, highlight the Insert option to reveal a sub-menu and click on the Table option to reveal the Insert Table window.
3.   Borders: click on the Format menu and the Borders and Shading option to reveal the Borders and Shading window. Alternatively select the Table Properties option within the Table menu.
4.   Bullets and lists: select the Format menu and the Bullets and Numbering option to open the Bullets and Numbering window.
5.   Footnotes and endnotes: select the Insert menu and highlight the Reference option to open an extra menu of four choices. Click on the Footnote option to open the Footnote and Endnote window.
6.   Margins: select the File menu and the Page Setup option to open the Page Setup window.
7.   Orientation: select the File menu and the Page Setup option to open the Page Setup window.

8.   Gutter: select the File menu and the Page Setup option to open the Page Setup window.

9.   Line spacing, alignment and paragraph indents: select the Format menu and the Paragraph option to open the Paragraph window and choose the Indents and Spacing tab.

10.   Pagination, widows and orphans, and hyphenation: select the Format menu and the Paragraph option to open the Paragraph window and choose the Line and Page Break tab.

11.   Columns: select the Format menu and the Columns option to reveal the Columns window.

12.   Images: select the Insert menu, highlight the Picture option to reveal eight further options which relate to inserting images including clip art, adding an image stored in a file, and inserting a scanned or photographed image.

13.   Draw toolbar: allows you to add clip art, insert a picture, create charts, rotate images, change the colour of areas, lines and text, and add shadow or three-dimensional effects to objects.

14.   Text box: within the draw toolbar and the Insert menu is the Text Box option.

15.   Windows® Paint: select the Start menu, highlight the Programs and Accessories option to reveal a list of accessories, and click on Paint.

16.   Caption: select the Insert menu, highlight Reference and click on Caption to open the Caption window.

17.   Index and Table: select the Insert menu, and highlight the Reference option to reveal additional options including Index and Table.

18. . Spelling and grammar: select the Tools menu and the Spelling and Grammar option.

19.   Thesaurus: select the Tools menu, highlight the Language choice to reveal a sub-menu including the option Thesaurus.

20.   Set language: select the Tools menu, highlight the Language choice to reveal a sub-menu including the option Set Language.

21.   Track changes: select the Tool menu and the option Track Changes to open a toolbox which allows you to choose what changes are shown and how.

22.   Find and replace: select the Edit menu and either the Find or the Replace options. The Find and Replace window will appear.

23.   Word count: select the Tools menu and the Word Count option.

24.   Font colour and highlighting: select icons on the formatting toolbar.

25   Hyperlink: select the Insert menu and the Hyperlink option to open the Insert Hyperlink window.

26.   Comment: position the cursor at the point where you would like the comment to be activated, then select the Insert menu and the Comment option.

27.   Printing: select the File menu and the Print option to open the Print window.

28.   Print preview: select the File menu and the Print Preview option to see the preview.

2 Working with numbers (Microsoft® Excel)

▶ Overview

Many courses involve the analysis of numerical information. This will often be the outcome of your own investigations, experiments or research. You will be required to demonstrate your skills in evaluating and investigating data in order to reach conclusions. Analysis can involve mathematical processes, visual comparison of data, or structured presentation using graphs and charts. This chapter will focus on assisting you to develop a foundation of appropriate skills relevant to your studies. It will include converting mathematical tables into charts and graphs to assist interpretation and presentation.

▶ Introduction

This chapter concentrates on the use of spreadsheets and charts and graphs to analyse and present numerical information. It covers:

- spreadsheets
- formatting
- sorting
- functions
- formulas
- replication
- referencing (relative and absolute)
- models
- analysing data
- presentation
- printing
- charts and graphs
- types of charts and graphs

- selecting appropriate charts and graphs
- creating
- editing (legend, colour, titles, captions and axes)
- drawing tools
- printing
- screen capture: editing in Paint and Word
- exporting charts and graphs to other documents.

The chapter is based on the spreadsheet application Microsoft® Excel, which is available in a variety of versions:

- Excel 95
- Excel 97
- Excel 2000
- Excel 2002.

You may be using any of these, since they represent the development of the product over the past nine years. People often purchase Microsoft® Office, which is a range of integrated products (word processing, spreadsheets, databases and so on). Microsoft® Office is again available in a range of versions (Office 95, Office 97, Office 2000 and Office 2002) that align with the version of the individual products. Microsoft® Office XP combines applications which are individually designated as Word 2002, Excel 2002 and so on. The techniques described in this chapter are based on Excel 2002. However, you will be able to transfer them to any version of Excel to which you have access, and hints and tips are provided to make this easier.

Figure 2.1 shows the Microsoft® Excel 2002 (Office XP) working area. This is similar to earlier versions of Excel except that the right-hand column is not displayed in the earlier versions.

▶ Formatting

Formatting is critical to the appearance of your spreadsheet, and will help you when you want to integrate it into reports on experiments, investigations or assignment documents. However, it is equally important that a clear easy-to-understand spreadsheet will help you avoid making errors either initially or months later when you are revising. What is obvious now may be less clear in six months' time.

Microsoft® Excel provides features with which you may be familiar if

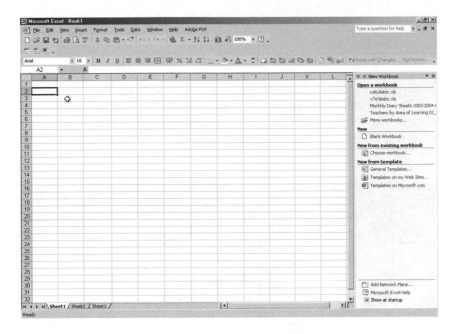

Figure 2.1 Microsoft® Excel

you have used Word or other Microsoft® Office applications. These include selecting:

- fonts
- character size
- justification
- bold text
- italics
- underlined text
- borders
- font colours.

These features are available from the formatting toolbar in the same way as they are provided in Word and earlier versions of Excel.

In addition Excel offers facilities to change the format of numbers, and the grid of rows and columns that make up the spreadsheet. These include:

- presenting numerical information in a currency format
- presenting numerical information as a percentage

- changing the number of decimal places that numbers show
- changing the width of columns
- changing the height of rows.

A number of formatting features are accessed via the formatting toolbar (Figure 2.2). This toolbar is the same in earlier versions of Microsoft® Excel (such as Excel 97). You highlight the numbers you want to change and then select the function.

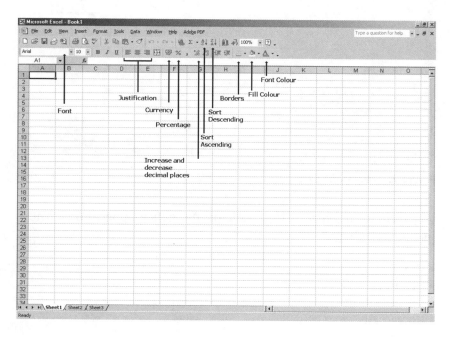

Figure 2.2 Formatting and Standard toolbar

The width of columns and the height of rows can be changed by:

1. Selecting the Format menu.
2. Highlighting either the Rows or Columns option to reveal additional options including Height and Width respectively. When these options are chosen, a window opens called either Row Height or Column Width.
3. Change the dimensions by simply inserting the new values. The rows and columns selected (that is, highlighted) will be changed.

Activity   Practising formatting

Create the spreadsheet below which shows the number of books borrowed from a college library by subject each week.

Subject	Week 1	Week 2	Week 3	Week 4
Science	56	69	24	75
Physics	12	21	32	11
History	82	90	75	70
Chemistry	36	28	22	27
Engineering	10	12	8	14
English	44	42	88	34

1. Embolden and centre the column headings.
2. Change the font of the row headings to Tahoma and the rest of the sheet to Arial.
3. Change the character size of the whole sheet to 12.
4. Adjust the row height and column width to improve the appearance of the spreadsheet.
5. Change the numbers so they all show two decimal places.

Feedback
Figure 2.3 shows the result.
   The fonts, emboldening, centring and decimal places were changed by highlighting the desired feature then selecting the function on the formatting toolbar.
   The width of the subject column was changed by dragging the column line so that the subject headings could fit neatly within the column. The other columns were all changed to a width of 10 by highlighting the week columns, selecting the Format menu, highlighting the Column option and choosing the Width option to open the window, then inserting the new value.

Subject	Week 1	Week 2	Week 3	Week 4
Science	56.00	69.00	24.00	75.00
Physics	12.00	21.00	32.00	11.00
History	82.00	90.00	75.00	70.00
Chemistry	36.00	28.00	22.00	27.00
Engineering	10.00	12.00	8.00	14.00
English	44.00	42.00	88.00	34.00

Figure 2.3 Library books spreadsheet

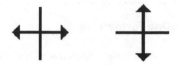

Figure 2.4 New pointer shape

An alternative to using the Format menu functions involves dragging the column and row lines to new positions by:

1. Positioning your mouse pointer over the line in the column or row heading (such as column A or row 23).When it is in position the pointer changes shape (see Figure 2.4, above).
2. Dragging the line to a new position by holding down the left mouse button.

Both methods of changing heights and widths are the same in earlier versions of Excel (such as Excel 97).

▶ Sorting

When considering a table of data, you will quite often need to sort it so that it is presented in ascending or descending order: that is, in alphabetical or reverse alphabetical order if you are dealing with text, or highest to lowest or its reverse if it is numerical information. This can be done in Excel using functions on the standard toolbar (Figure 2.2). The standard toolbar is similar in earlier versions of Excel (such as Excel 97), and the sorting icons are identical.

▶ Formulas

There will be occasions when you need to analyse mathematical information as part of your studies. For example, you might be investigating the results of an assignment to identify people's attitudes, or the outcomes of a physics experiment. Spreadsheets are designed to undertake a wide range of mathematical calculations and analysis. They are ideal when you have a lot of numerical information to consider, and are particularly effective in helping you consider the effects of changing variables. You always need to check that your formulas are correct, but once this is established,

Activity   Sorting

Using the library spreadsheet you created in the previous activity, sort the table to present the information in descending and then ascending order.

Feedback
The results are shown in Figure 2.5. They were achieved by highlighting the table and choosing the descending icon and then the ascending icon.

Descending

Subject	Week 1	Week 2	Week 3	Week 4
Science	56.00	69.00	24.00	75.00
Physics	12.00	21.00	32.00	11.00
History	82.00	90.00	75.00	70.00
English	44.00	42.00	88.00	34.00
Engineering	10.00	12.00	8.00	14.00
Chemistry	36.00	28.00	22.00	27.00

Ascending

Subject	Week 1	Week 2	Week 3	Week 4
Chemistry	36.00	28.00	22.00	27.00
Engineering	10.00	12.00	8.00	14.00
English	44.00	42.00	88.00	34.00
History	82.00	90.00	75.00	70.00
Physics	12.00	21.00	32.00	11.00
Science	56.00	69.00	24.00	75.00

Figure 2.5 Sorting

the accuracy of your results is guaranteed. This is helpful if you have a series of assignments to analyse or a large amount of data.

Microsoft® Excel is a modern spreadsheet that is widely used in business and education. It uses the following mathematical operators in all versions:

+   add
−   subtract
*   multiply
/   divide
<   less than
<=   less than or equal to
>   more than
>=   greater than or equal to

These operators can manipulate the contents of spreadsheet cells to carry out mathematical calculations.

Example

=C5–F7	Subtracts the contents of cell F7 from the contents of C5.
=C6+G8	Adds the contents of cell C6 to those of cell G8.
=H5/J11	Divides the contents of cell H5 by the contents of cell J11.
=A11*A13	Multiplies the contents of cell A11 by the contents of cell A13.

These straightforward examples can be built up to undertake more complex mathematical actions. The equals sign at the start of each formula instructs Excel to carry out the calculation.

Example

=C5-F7+C6/A2	Subtracts the contents of cell F7 from the contents of cell C5 and then adds the result of dividing the contents of cell C6 by cell A2 to the total.

Excel also uses brackets so that any calculation within brackets is resolved first before the remainder of the calculation is carried out.

Example

=(A12+D6)*F5	Adds the contents of cells A12 and D6 and multiplies the total by contents of F5.
=(M3*V3)-(T4/G2)	Multiplies the contents of cell M3 by the contents of cell V3 and subtracts from this total the contents of cell T4 divided by the contents of cell G2.

Formulas can contain a number of different mathematical operators (such as add, subtract, multiply and divide). Excel works out multiplication and division first, and addition and subtraction second. If the formula contains several multiplications and divisions, and/or additions and subtractions, it performs the calculations from left to right. Of course, any part of the calculation enclosed in brackets is calculated first. The mathematical rules are the same in earlier versions of Excel.

Activity   Mathematical operations

The data below are the results of an experiment to investigate how a rod of metal expands as temperature increases.

Temperature (degrees C)	Increase in length of rod (millimetres)
20	0.00
35	0.78
40	2.34
45	3.13
50	4.06
55	4.69
60	5.47
65	6.25
70	7.03
75	7.81
80	8.59
85	9.38
90	10.16

1. Enter the data into your spreadsheet.
2. Create a third column showing the change in length for each degree rise in temperature, using a formula for each step change in temperature (increase in length divided by temperature change). So your results should look like:

Temperature (degrees C)	Increase in length of rod (millimetres)	Change in length per degree change
20	0.00	0.00
35	0.78	0.052

Feedback
Figure 2.6 shows the spreadsheet, and Figure 2.7 illustrates the formulas. To calculate the change in length caused by each one degree rise in temperature, you need to divide the increase in length by the rise in temperature. In this case it is necessary to subtract B4, the initial temperature, from B5, the first increased temperature, to obtain the first rise in temperature, and to subtract C4, the initial length, from C5 the next length, to obtain the first change in length, and so on down the table. If you had any difficulty doing this, use the formulas in Figure 2.7 to guide you. ▶

Activity Mathematical operations – *continued*

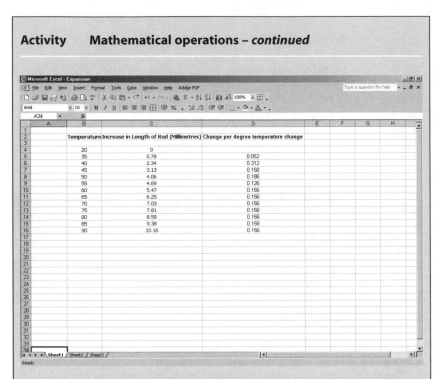

Figure 2.6 Spreadsheet for change in length of rod

Increase in length of rod (millimeters)	Change per degree temperature change
0	
0.78	= (C5–C4)/(B5–B4)
2.34	= (C6–C5)/(B6–B5)
3.13	= (C7–C6)/(B7–B6)
4.06	= (C8–C7)/(B8–B7)
4.69	= (C9–C8)/(B9–B8)
5.47	= (C10–C9)/(B10–B9)
6.25	= (C11–C10)/(B11–B10)
7.03	= (C12–C11)/(B12–B11)
7.81	= (C13–C12)/(B13–B12)
8.59	= (C14–C13)/(B14–B13)
9.38	= (C15–C14)/(B15–B14)
10.16	= (C16–C15)/(B16–B15)
0	

Figure 2.7 Formulas for the spreadsheet in Figure 2.6

Standard functions

You can develop any number of formulas using the mathematical operators, but to help you, many spreadsheets offer standard functions to sum columns or rows of numbers, obtain average figures and carry out numerous other operations. Standard functions include:

SUM	Sums the contents of a column or row of numbers.
AVERAGE	Produces the average of a column or row of numbers.
SQRT	Calculates the square root of the contents of a cell (for example, =SQRT(D5) produces the square root of D5).
IF	Allows you specify that an action is only undertaken if the condition is satisfied. You can use IF to produce complex conditions (for example, IF (F7 <40, Fail) means that if the contents of cell F7 is less than 40 then the word Fail should be shown).
STDEV	Estimates the standard deviation (for example STDEV(D5: D16) obtains the standard deviation of the values in cells D5 to D16).
CHITEST	gives the value of a chi squared test.

Range

Many functions require that you specify the cells on which they will operate, called the *range* of cells. In the examples below, the range of cells is identified by writing the addresses of the first and last cells, separated by a colon to designate that all the cells between the two are included. The range is then enclosed in brackets.

Examples

=SUM(D5:D12)	Totals the contents of the cells D5, D6, D7, D8, D9, D10, D11 and D12.
=AVERAGE (D5:D12)	Averages the contents of the cells (D5, D6, D7, D8, D9, D10, D11 and D12). This is the equivalent of writing (D5+D6+D7+ D8+D9+D10+D11+D12)/8.

A complete list of all the functions can be accessed by clicking on the function button on the standard toolbar to reveal a drop-down menu. This is the same in earlier versions of Excel (such as Excel 97) except that the Paste function window appears when the button is clicked, and this contains the standard functions. If you click on the More Functions

Activity   Mathematical functions

Table 2.1 shows the results of an investigation into the flow of traffic through a village at set times over a 24-hour period.

Table 2.1 Traffic flow

Time	Motor bikes	Cars	Lorries
1	0	2	0
2	0	3	1
3	0	2	1
4	1	3	1
5	2	6	2
6	3	15	3
7	5	55	4
8	4	75	3
9	3	45	5
10	2	32	6
11	1	22	9
12	2	11	2
13	1	7	7
14	3	7	5
15	2	4	3
16	2	5	3
17	4	15	2
18	5	71	1
19	3	12	0
20	1	8	0
21	1	4	1
22	2	5	0
23	1	3	0
24	0	2	0

1. Create a spreadsheet based on this information.
2. Total the three traffic flow columns and the 24 rows using the SUM function.
3. Find the average number of motorbikes, cars and lorries over the 24-hour period using the AVERAGE function.
4. Find the average number of vehicles for each hour of the period and the average overall using the AVERAGE function.

Feedback
Figure 2.8 shows the final spreadsheet. You can enter the function ranges from the keyboard, or indicate them by highlighting then selecting the function (for example, highlight C4 to C29 and select the SUM function). The program total carries out the calculation and puts the answer in the cell in which the function is entered (cell C29 in this case).

Figure 2.9 shows the formulas used.

Activity Mathematical functions – *continued*

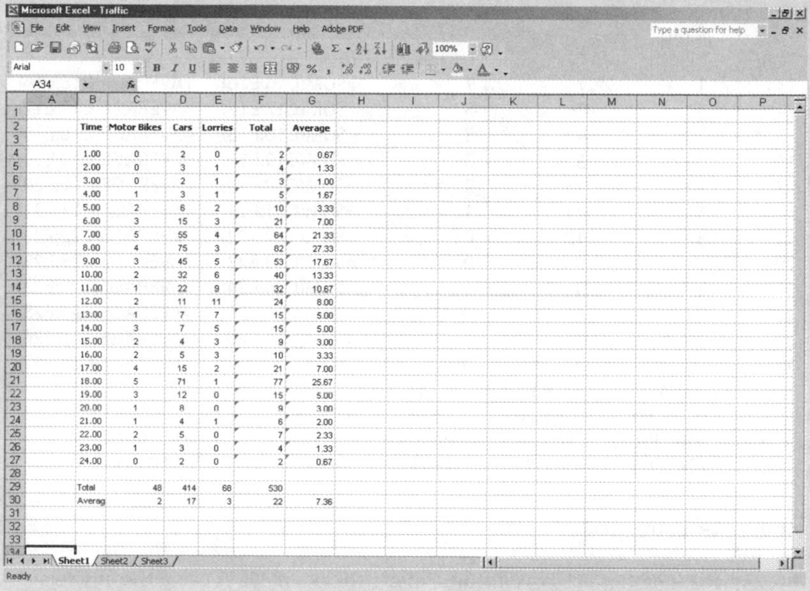

Time	Motor Bikes	Cars	Lorries	Total	Average
1.00	0	2	0	2	0.67
2.00	0	3	1	4	1.33
3.00	0	2	1	3	1.00
4.00	1	3	1	5	1.67
5.00	2	6	2	10	3.33
6.00	3	15	3	21	7.00
7.00	5	55	4	64	21.33
8.00	4	75	3	82	27.33
9.00	3	45	5	53	17.67
10.00	2	32	6	40	13.33
11.00	1	22	9	32	10.67
12.00	2	11	11	24	8.00
13.00	1	7	7	15	5.00
14.00	3	7	5	15	5.00
15.00	2	4	3	9	3.00
16.00	2	5	3	10	3.33
17.00	4	15	2	21	7.00
18.00	5	71	1	77	25.67
19.00	3	12	0	15	5.00
20.00	1	8	0	9	3.00
21.00	1	4	1	6	2.00
22.00	2	5	0	7	2.33
23.00	1	3	0	4	1.33
24.00	0	2	0	2	0.67
Total	48	414	68	530	
Averag	2	17	3	22	7.36

Figure 2.8 Traffic flow spreadsheet

Time	Motor bikes	Cars	Lorries	Total	Average
1	0	2	0	=SUM(C4:E4)	=AVERAGE(C4:E4)
2	0	3	1	=SUM(C5:E5)	=AVERAGE(C5:E5)
3	0	2	1	=SUM(C6:E6)	=AVERAGE(C6:E6)
4	1	3	1	=SUM(C7:E7)	=AVERAGE(C7:E7)
5	2	6	2	=SUM(C8:E8)	=AVERAGE(C8:E8)
6	3	15	3	=SUM(C9:E9)	=AVERAGE(C9:E9)
7	5	55	4	=SUM(C10:E10)	=AVERAGE(C10:E10)
8	4	75	3	=SUM(C11:E11)	=AVERAGE(C11:E11)
9	3	45	5	=SUM(C12:E12)	=AVERAGE(C12:E12)
10	2	32	6	=SUM(C13:E13)	=AVERAGE(C13:E13)
11	1	22	9	=SUM(C14:E14)	=AVERAGE(C14:E14)
12	2	11	11	=SUM(C15:E15)	=AVERAGE(C15:E15)

Figure 2.9 Formulas for traffic flow spreadsheet *(continued on page 54)*

Activity   Mathematical functions – *continued*

Time	Motor bikes	Cars	Lorries	Total	Average
13	1	7	7	=SUM(C16:E16)	=AVERAGE(C16:E16)
14	3	7	5	=SUM(C17:E17)	=AVERAGE(C17:E17)
15	2	4	3	=SUM(C18:E18)	=AVERAGE(C18:E18)
16	2	5	3	=SUM(C19:E19)	=AVERAGE(C19:E19)
17	4	15	2	=SUM(C20:E20)	=AVERAGE(C20:E20)
18	5	71	1	=SUM(C21:E21)	=AVERAGE(C21:E21)
19	3	12	0	=SUM(C22:E22)	=AVERAGE(C22:E22)
20	1	8	0	=SUM(C23:E23)	=AVERAGE(C23:E23)
21	1	4	1	=SUM(C24:E24)	=AVERAGE(C24:E24)
22	2	5	0	=SUM(C25:E25)	=AVERAGE(C25:E25)
23	1	3	0	=SUM(C26:E26)	=AVERAGE(C26:E26)
24	0	2	0	=SUM(C27:E27)	=AVERAGE(C27:E27)
Total	=SUM (C4:C28)	=SUM (D4:D28)	=SUM (E4:E28)	=SUM (F4:F28)	
Average	=AVERAGE (C4:C27)	=AVERAGE (D4:D27)	=AVERAGE (E4:E27)	=AVERAGE (F4:F27)	=AVERAGE (G4:G29)

Figure 2.9 continued

If you have found this activity difficult, explore the possibilities using the answers provided until you are confident.

option in the drop-down menu, the Insert window is revealed with a full list of functions. The definition of each function is given at the bottom of the window.

▶ Replication

In many applications you can copy information and then paste it into a new location. This is also true of all versions of Microsoft® Excel. In a spreadsheet the location is often important, especially when it forms part of a formula or function. Copying in a spreadsheet is called *replication*. Formulas and functions will adjust to take account of their new position.

Example
Copying =SUM(C4:C28) from the C column, where it is summing the

contents of the cells in the range C4 to C28 inclusive, to the D column will change the formula to read =SUM(D4:D28). The formula is changed to adjust to the new position.

Replication also happens when you insert a new row or column, delete them or alter the spreadsheet in any way. The formula will be modified by the change. The next section on referencing will continue to develop this theme.

▶ Referencing (relative and absolute)

When developing a spreadsheet, it is vital to be able to stipulate the location. This can be a single cell (such as A4, to indicate the cell at column A and row 4) or an area of the sheet (such as A4:A9, to indicate the A column between rows 4 and 9 inclusive). When the location is part of a formula or function, it is known as a *reference*. References are categorized as either relative or absolute.

Relative
A relative reference is essentially the standard one of Excel, and you do not need to do anything particular to create it. If you replicate an area of the sheet, the reference will alter to take account of the new position.

Absolute
The opposite of a relative reference is one that does not change when replication takes place. The reference is known as an absolute. Unlike a relative reference where you do not have to take any action to create one, you must indicate if a reference is to be absolute. To do this, you use the $ symbol.

Example

| Relative reference | =AVERAGE (F12: F34) |
| Absolute reference | =AVERAGE ($F$12: $F$34) |

It is possible to have both relative and absolute references in the same formula. This is known as *mixed referencing*.

When developing formulas you may want to use relative references to enable you to copy formulas to new parts of the sheet and ensure they are accurate. If you enter the formula from the keyboard there is always the possibility of making an error. The use of absolute references is not so obvious, but they can prove useful if you want to employ a standard value in a formula.

Example of an absolute reference
If cell A1 contains the standard value for VAT (say, 17.5%), this can be used throughout the spreadsheet to calculate tax due. When the rate changes, a single amendment will allow the whole sheet to be updated.

► Models

You can use spreadsheets for a variety of purposes, from a simple presentation of information through to calculating a range of results. However, a major role for a spreadsheet is to provide a mathematical model, enabling you to explore the outcomes when making a range of changes. It therefore answers the question 'What if ...?' (that is, what happens when a variable is changed). The activity below offers you the opportunity to explore a straightforward mathematical model.

The two activities produce models which are about predicting the consequences of a change in the two activities, changes in price and interest rate respectively.

► Analysing data

Analysis fundamentally involves comparing different information in a way that makes it possible to identify trends, changes and anomalies. It requires data to be reviewed systematically. There are a variety of ways of analysing information including:

- calculating the mean or average value so that other values can be compared to it
- turning values into percentages so that comparisons are more easy carried out
- using statistical tests such as standard deviation
- using charts and graphs to provide a visual comparison (we consider this later in the chapter).

Activity   Models

This activity concerns modelling the management of a car wash to consider what effect changes in price would have on profits. The owners know that as the price increases, the demand for the car wash decreases, and they have developed a mathematical formula to express the relationship. The formula is:

No. of customers = 230000 – 3200 * price (in pounds)

The car wash has both fixed and variable costs. Variable costs are calculated by multiplying the unit cost by demand. The unit cost is that of washing a single car, and is £1.20.

Profit is calculated by subtracting the total cost (that is, both fixed and variable costs) from the revenue.

Create a model of the car wash profits and consider the effects of charging £1, £2, £3 , £4 and £5 for a car wash.

Feedback
Figure 2.10 gives the data for a spreadsheet that models the car wash, and Figure 2.11 shows the formulas. These show that as price increases, so does profit, until a price of £5 is reached, when profits start to fall. A manager basing prices on this model would charge about £4 for each car wash to maximize profit.

Car wash

Price (£)	1	2	3	4	5
Demand	16800	13600	10400	7200	4000
Revenue	16800	27200	31200	28800	20000
Variable costs	20160	16320	12480	8640	4800
Fixed costs	7500	7500	7500	7500	7500
Unit cost	1.2	1.2	1.2	1.2	1.2
Profit	–10860	3380	11220	12660	7700

Figure 2.10 Car wash model

Car wash

Price (£)	1	2	3	4	5
Demand	=20000– 3200*C5	=20000–1 3200*D5	=20000– 3200*E5	=20000– 3200*F5	=20000– 3200*G5
Revenue	=C5*C6	=D5*D6	=E5*E6	=F5*F6	=G5*G6
Variable costs	=C10*C6	=D10*D6	=E10*E6	=F10*F6	=G10*G6
Fixed costs	7500	7500	7500	7500	7500
Unit cost	1.2	1.2	1.2	1.2	1.2
Profit	=C7–C8–C9	=D7–D8–D9	=E7–E8–E9	=F7–F8–F9	=G7–G8–G9

Figure 2.11 Formulas for car wash model

Activity   Buying a car

This is a second modelling activity based around the repayments on loans for car purchase. The key factors are:

1. Size of the loan.
2. Length of loan in months.
3. Interest rate (annual).
4. Monthly repayment.

Monthly repayments are equal to (interest rate/100 multiplied by the loan) divided by length of loan, plus loan divided by length of loan.

Consider the effects of borrowing £10,000 over 60 months at interest rates of 6%, 8%, 10% and 12%. What would be the effects on the monthly repayments?

Feedback
Figure 2.12 shows the information for a spreadsheet to model the car loan. It shows the growth in monthly repayments and the total repayments as the interest rate increases. This helps you to make a choice between rates. Figure 2.13 again shows the formulas used.

Car loan

Interest rate (%)	6	8	10	12
Size of loan (£)	10000	10000	10000	10000
Length of Loan (months)	60	60	60	60
Repayments (monthly) (£)	176.6667	180	183.3333	186.6667
Total repaid (£)	10600	10800	11000	11200

Figure 2.12 Car loan model

Car loan

Interest rate (%)	6	8	10	12
Size of loan (£)	10000	10000	10000	10000
Length of loan (months)	60	60	60	60
Repayments (monthly) (£)	=(C5/100*C6)/ C7+C6/C7	=(D5/100*D6)/ D7+D6/D7	=(E5/100*E6)/ E7+E6/E7	=(F5/100*F6)/ F7+F6/F7
Total repaid (£)	=C8*C7	=D8*D7	=E8*E7	=F8*F7

Figure 2.13 Formulas for car loan model

Activity   Analysis of trade union membership

Table 2.2 shows a breakdown by job of the employees who are members of a trade union within an organisation.

Table 2.2 Trade union membership

	Managers	Office staff	Shop floor
Member	5	44	106
Non-member	12	76	14

Create a spreadsheet and analyse the information. You might want to look at:

1. Total of each occupation, members and non-members.
2. Percentage of each occupational area who are members of a trade union.
3. Percentage of employees who are members.

Feedback
Figure 2.14 shows the information, and Figure 2.15 the formulas, for a spreadsheet in which the total number of trade union members is calculated using the SUM function, the total number of each occupation is calculated using a formula (=C6+C8), and percentages of members in each occupation and in the whole organization are calculated using a formula and percentage function.

Once you have completed this straightforward analysis you can see that a large majority (88 per cent) of the shop floor are members of a trade union, while relatively few managers are members, but overall a majority of employees are members. With information in a percentage form you can compare membership in another organization more clearly than by using the simple numbers.

	Manager	Office staff	Shop floor	Total
Members	5	44	106	155
Percentage members	29	37	88	60
Non-members	12	76	14	102
Percentage non-members	71	63	12	40
Total	17	120	120	257

Figure 2.14 Trade union membership

Activity   Analysis of trade union membership – *continued*

	Manager	Office staff	Shop floor	Total
Members	5	44	106	=SUM(C6:F6)
Percentage members	=C6/C10	=D6/D10	=E6/E10	=G6/G10
Non-members	12	76	14	=SUM(C8:F8)
Percentage non-members	=C8/C10	=D8/D10	=E8/E10	=G8/G10
Total	=C6+C8	=D6+D8	=E6+E8	=SUM(C10:F10)

Figure 2.15 Formulas for trade union membership

► Linking spreadsheets

It is sometimes important to link spreadsheets. This involves transferring information from one sheet to another. This allows you to create complex models in which individual sheets focus on specific issues and transfer key information to other spreadsheets.

Earlier we created a spreadsheet for a car wash business, and included a value for the unit cost. This is calculated by considering the cost of the electricity, water and detergent required to wash a car. It will change with these variables, so it would be useful to create another spreadsheet and transfer the unit cost value to our original sheet.

The new sheet is created as sheet 2 in the same workbook. Figure 2.18 shows the new sheet.

To link the unit cost to sheet 1 of the original spreadsheet, select a cell (for instance, C9) and copy it by selecting the Edit menu and the Copy option. Move to the original spreadsheet (which is known as the dependent sheet), then select the Edit menu and the Paste Special option. This will open the Paste Special window. Click the Paste Link button. Now as the value of the unit cost changes, it will change the value in the original sheet. This dynamic link is very useful as it allows you to extend the model by considering the effects of three core costs (electricity, water and detergent). When you make the link you will see that a formula is created on the formula line, that is, =Sheet2!$C$9 which indicates that the value is sheet 2 cell C9, and it is an absolute value to prevent it being changed by copying.

Entering a formula is another way of creating a link.

Figure 2.19 shows the new sheet.

Activity   Analysis of workforce

Table 2.3 shows a breakdown of the ages and genders of employees in an organization.

Table 2.3 Analysis of workforce

Age	Male	Female
16 –25	5	10
26 –35	25	20
36–45	35	40
46–55	20	20
56–65	15	10

Analyse this information. You may want to:

- produce a total of employees in each age band
- calculate the percentage of employees in each age band
- identify the age band with the largest group of men and women

Feedback
A sample analysis is shown in Figure 2.16, with the formulas used in Figure 2.17.

Age	Male	Female	Total	Percentage
16–25	5	10	15	8%
26–35	25	20	45	23%
36–45	35	40	75	38%
46–55	20	20	40	20%
56–65	15	10	25	13%
Total	100	100	200	

Figure 2.16 Age profile analysis

Age	Male	Female	Total	Percentage
16 –25	5	10	=SUM(D5:E5)	=F5/F15
26 –35	25	20	=SUM(D7:E7)	=F7/F15
36 –45	35	40	=SUM(D9:E9)	=F9/F15
46 –55	20	20	=SUM(D11:E11)	=F11/F15
56 –65	15	10	=SUM(D13:E13)	=F13/F15
Total	=SUM(D5:D14)	=SUM(E5:E14)	=SUM(F5:F14)	

Figure 2.17 Formulas for age profile analysis

A	B	C	D
1			
2			
3	Unit Cost		
4			
5	Electricity	0.6	
6	Detergent	0.35	
7	Water	0.25	
8			
9	Total	1.2	
10			

Figure 2.18 Unit cost calculation for car wash

	A	B	C	D	E	F	G	H
1								
2								
3		**Car wash**	**Amount**					
4								
5		Price (£)	1	2	3	4	6	
6		Demand	16800	13600	10400	7200	4000	
7		Revenue	16800	27200	31200	28800	20000	
8		Variable costs	20160	16320	12480	8640	4800	
9		Fixed costs	7500	7500	7500	7500	7500	
10		Unit cost	1.2	1.2	1.2	1.2	1.2	
11		Profit	−10860	3380	11220	12660	7700	
12								

Figure 2.19 Linking spreadsheets

▶ Presentation

Spreadsheets can be copied and pasted into Word, and also imported using the File option in the Insert menu. This can be useful when you are writing up an assignment, producing a report of an experiment or writing a longer document. It is important to be able to adjust the presentation of your spreadsheet so that readers can understand the information. A spreadsheet can be used simply to present information in a tabular way, again making its appearance a critical factor. However, you may want to print the sheet in order to insert it as an additional page within your work. We consider printing spreadsheets on page 71.

Columns and rows

A useful way to improve the appearance of a sheet is to add or delete columns and rows. This is also important when you want to amend an existing sheet. Readability is often enhanced by the effective use of white space. To add a row or column:

1. Highlight a row or column by clicking on the title area. You will notice the pointer changes shape to an arrow and the column and row change colour.
2. Select the Insert menu and the Column or Row option. The column will be added to the right of the highlighted one. The row will be added below the highlighted one. It is an identical process in earlier versions of Excel.

Borders
Areas of your spreadsheet can be enclosed in a border to improve its appearance. To add a border:

1. Select the View menu.
2. Highlight the Toolbar option.
3. Choose Borders to open the Borders window. This is not available in earlier versions of Excel, where you need to use the Borders icon on the formatting toolbar to access the function. The Borders window provides four functions. They are:
   • Draw a border with a pencil tool.
   • Draw a grid.
   • Select line colour.
   • Select style of line.
   The drawing tool allows you to select where the border will be drawn. The grid option will include the cell borders as well as an area.

An alternative approach is to use the Border icon on the formatting toolbar (see Figure 2.2). This includes an option Outside Border which will enclose a highlighted area with a border or grid.

Colour
Excel not only offers the option of a coloured border, but you can also change the background and text colours. These options are available from the formatting toolbar (Figure 2.2) and are called Fill and Font Color. The Fill Color icon allows you to fill a highlighted area with your selected colour. The Font Color will change the colour of any highlighted text. These functions are available in earlier versions of Excel (such as Excel 97).

▶ Charts and graphs

While a table can be a useful way to present numerical information, a chart or graph can prove even more powerful. Pictures are often more attractive and easier to understand than a table. In the presentation activity you created a table of information illustrating the book loans from a library subject by subject. This enables you to compare the different subjects, but it is not easy since there are six subjects to compare over a four-week period. Data transformed into a chart would be much easier to consider. Figure 2.21 shows one way of presenting the information, with each subject shown as a coloured bar and grouped by week.

Charts and graphs created by Excel can be copied into other Microsoft® Office documents. They are a form of analysis in that they

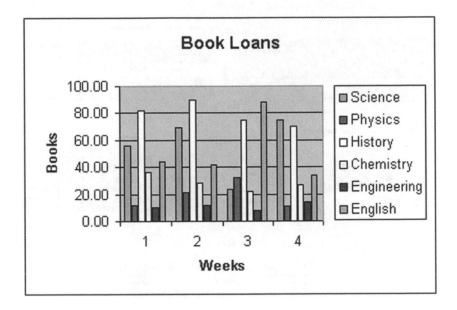

Figure 2.21 Book loans chart

compare and contrast information, and they can add visual impact to your documents.

Types of charts and graphs

Microsoft® Excel provides you with functions to produce a variety of charts and graphs. The main types are:

- column charts
- pie charts
- bar charts
- line graphs
- scatter graphs.

These can be produced in either two or three dimensions, and also in a range of variations on the main types. Figure 2.22 illustrates the five main types for week 1 of the book loans spreadsheet. Compare the different charts and graphs and the information you are presented with, then decide which one you prefer. The choice of chart or graph depends on what you want to present. You need to consider what you hope to achieve.

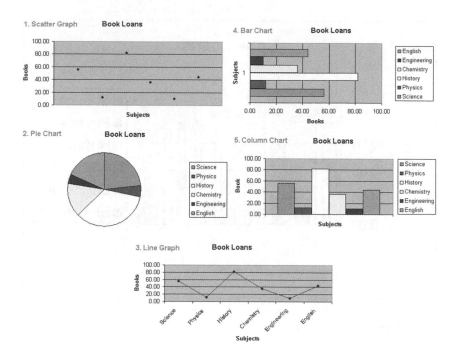

Figure 2.22 Chart examples

The prime function of charts and graphs is to enable you to compare and contrast numerical information. You can:

- compare one factor with others (such as rainfall in one country with rainfall in other parts of the world): column, pie and bar charts are often useful for this type of use
- consider how an item changes over time (for example, cars travelling along a road each hour during the day) – a line graph is often effective in this case
- look at how one variable changes in relation to another (such as sales compared with price) – a scatter graph is often an option here.

Creating a chart or graph

The process of creating a chart or graph is straightforward, and Excel provides ways to edit the resulting display. You can produce a chart or graph of either a whole spreadsheet or a part. In either case you need to:

1. Highlight the area you want to consider.

2. Select the Insert menu and then the Chart option. This will open the Chart Wizard which takes you through the process step by step. This is available in earlier versions of Microsoft® Excel (such as Excel 97). Figure 2.23 illustrates the opening display. The top line of the Chart Wizard indicates that it is the first step of four. Each step has a number of choices shown by the tabs at the top of the window. Figure 2.23 shows a list of chart types, with an extra tab providing more. On the right-hand side of the display are examples of the type highlighted in the list on the left. A range of options is provided, from which you select by clicking on the option of your choice. You make a final choice with the Next button at the bottom of the right-hand side of the window.

3. Click on the button 'Press and Hold to View Sample' to see a sample of your selected chart in order to ensure it is suitable before you select the Next button.

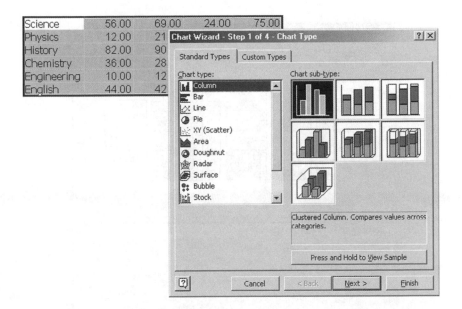

Figure 2.23 Chart Wizard opening display

4. Click on the Next button to move to the second step, shown in Figure 2.24. This gives you a view of the chart, and tells you the data range and whether it has a row or column view. It is always worth considering both row and column views.

5. Click on the radio button (i.e. Rows or Columns – Figure 2.24) to display changes so you can inspect them and select the most appropriate one. The data range indicates the area of the spreadsheet included in the chart. In this example it is = Sheet1!$B$4:$F$9. This tells you the rectangular area covers from cell B4 in the top left-hand corner to cell F9 in the bottom right-hand corner. You can edit this area by changing the range, but it is often easier to return to the original spreadsheet and highlight a new area. The step 2 window has a tab called Series which enables you to edit the series. In this example, the series is the data relating to the four weeks, so you could remove the column for any of the weeks if you wanted, or add a column if you only included some weeks originally. There is also an option to change the name of the series. In this example it would be more meaningful to call the columns Week 1 to 4 respectively, rather than Series 1 to 4. Make your choices.

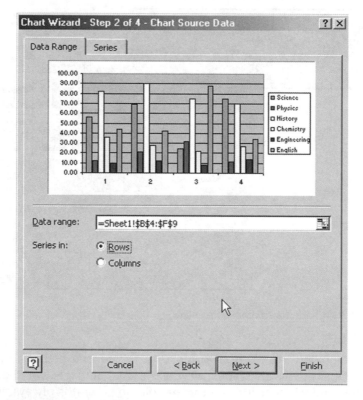

Figure 2.24 Chart Wizard step 2

6. Click on the <u>N</u>ext button to move to the third step, shown in Figure 2.25. This provides a range of choices enabling you to produce a chart that meets your needs. There are six tabs across the top of the window. Use the Titles tab to add a chart title. For this chart 'Book loans' has been chosen. You can also label the X and Y axes. Here they are called 'Subject' and 'Books'. Once you have entered the labels, they appear in the display on the right-hand side of the window. The other tabs are:

- Axes: to edit the axes (for example, change the scale)
- Gridlines: to insert or remove gridlines from the chart or graph
- Legend (key to the colour codes for the subjects): to place the legend in different positions with respect to the chart
- Data Labels: to add labels to the data displaycd on thc chart
- Data Table: to add a table of the spreadsheet data on to the chart.

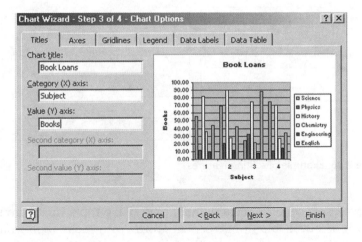

Figure 2.25 Chart Wizard step 3

7. Click on the <u>N</u>ext button to move to the fourth step once you have made your choices. This window lets you name your chart and insert it into the spreadsheet or another sheet.
8. Click on the <u>F</u>inish button once you have made your choices, and your chart will appear.

Editing

Having produced a graph or chart, you still have the option to edit many of its features such as:

- legend
- colour
- titles
- captions and axes.

In order to edit a particular feature of the chart, double-click on it. The feature will be highlighted, and the appropriate format window will open. This process is the same in earlier versions of Microsoft® Excel (such as Excel 97). Figure 2.26 shows an example. Notice that the feature is highlighted with small black squares.

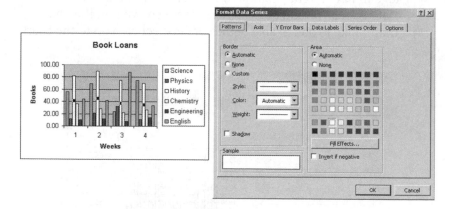

Figure 2.26 Example of editing features

Microsoft® Excel provides a number of drawing tools which are similar to those available in Microsoft® Word. With these tools you can add rectangles, autoshapes, ovals and wordart, insert clipart into the spreadsheets, and change colours. These allow you to enhance the presentation of the sheet and the chart.

Export charts and graphs
Once you have created a chart or graph you can export it into another Microsoft® Office file by simply copying and pasting it. The process is:

1. Highlight the chart.
2. Select the Edit menu and the Copy option.
3. Paste the chart into your chosen document.

▶ **Printing**

Spreadsheets, charts and graphs are often viewed and used on the screen, but printing them can be useful when you want to present the information or discuss models in a group. The key to printing a sheet is to consider how it will appear on paper. Excel provides a function called Print Preview in which you can consider the printed appearance of your chart:

1. Select the File menu.
2. Select the Print Preview option. The sheet will be displayed as if printed. You can then adjust it if necessary.

Print Preview provides a view of the printout, but to change the sheet you need to use functions such as Page Setup. To access this:

1. Select the File menu.
2. Choose the Page Setup option to open the Page Setup window. This allows you to scale the sheet to fit pages, change the presentation to portrait or landscape, alter margins and add headers or footers. You can also print with the sheet gridlines. These functions are also available in earlier versions of Microsoft® Excel (such as Excel 97).

Top tips

1. **Presentation:** Spreadsheets allow you to present numerical tables of data. They offer all the formatting functions of a word processor combined with many additional table features.
2. **Mathematical analysis:** Once you have established that your mathematical model of data is correct, you have a powerful tool for analysis, but always check that it is working correctly before using the model.
3. **Charts and graphs:** Turning mathematical tables of information into visual charts and graphs provides both a useful way of presenting your data and an additional form of analysis.

▶ Summary

1. Formatting: highlight the area and select the desired function from the formatting toolbar.

2. Number formatting: highlight the number (row or column) and select the function from the formatting toolbar.

3. Width of columns and height of rows: select the Format menu and then highlight either the Rows or Columns option to reveal additional options including Height and Width, respectively.

4. Sorting: highlight the row and select either the ascending or descending icon on the standard toolbar.

5. Functions: select the function button on the standard toolbar to reveal a drop-down menu.

6. Replication: select the Edit menu and the Copy or Paste option.

7. References: distinguish between relative references such as =AVERAGE (F12: F34) and absolute references such as =AVERAGE ($F$12: $F$34).

8. Add a row or column: highlight them then select the Insert menu and the Column or Row option. The column will be added to the right of the highlighted one. The row will be added below the highlighted one.

9. Linking sheets: select the cell and copy it by selecting the Edit menu and the Copy option. Move to the original spreadsheet (which is known as the dependent sheet) and then select the Edit menu and the Paste Special option. This will open the Paste Special window. Click the Paste Link button.

10. Border: select the View menu, highlight the Toolbar option and choose Borders to open the Borders window.

11. Create a chart or graph: highlight the area of the spreadsheet and select the Insert menu then the Chart option. This will open the Chart Wizard which will take you through the process step by step.

12. Edit chart or graph: double-click on the chart feature to highlight it and open the appropriate format window.

13. Copy and paste: highlight the chart then select the Edit menu and the Copy option. You can then paste it into your chosen document.

14. Page setup: select the File menu and Page Setup option.

15. Print preview: select the File menu and Print Preview option.

3 Communication (Microsoft Outlook®)

▶ Overview

Two of the most important study skills that you require to be a successful student are time management and communication. You need to manage your time effectively, organize yourself to achieve current and future objectives, and communicate in an appropriate way with your tutors and colleagues. Communication systems such as Microsoft Outlook® can assist you to manage your studies effectively from the outset.

▶ Introduction

This chapter will help you make the most of communication technology for your education (such as communicating with tutors and other students, sending assignments as attachments, and taking part in online discussions). It will also assist you to cope with some of the problems associated with e-mail such as junk mail or spam. The chapter will cover:

- advantages of e-mail
- e-mail systems
- netiquette
- virtual learning environments
- e-mail (sending, forwarding, receiving and organizing)
- address book
- mailgroups.

Electronic communications have already significantly changed the way education is supported and delivered. Many colleges and universities now make extensive use of e-mail, websites and other online resources.

Some of the main online approaches are:

- course materials available online (such as lecture notes, study guides and timetables)
- submitting assignments electronically
- feedback on assignments
- individual student records
- student discussion groups (to discuss particular aspects of the course and to seek help from peers)
- access to library catalogue
- communication with tutors.

Microsoft Outlook® is a sophisticated application which, in addition to helping you communicate, also provides you with the means to organize yourself. It enables you to develop a study plan/timetable, electronic reminders, lists of tasks and notes.

▶ Advantages of e-mail for education

E-mail can help you communicate with your tutors, fellow students and other college staff. It has numerous advantages but also some limitations. Table 3.1 summarizes the advantages and disadvantages of e-mail for education.

▶ E-mail systems

There are several ways to access e-mail. As part of an Internet Service Provider's (ISP's) service you will be provided with one or more e-mail accounts, and many World Wide Web functions offer free e-mail. Your college is also likely to provide you with an e-mail account. You can have several accounts with different addresses, and many users have different accounts for different purposes such as a private account for personal correspondence and a public account to register for online contacts. (This is very useful since spam is often received as a result of registering for online services and information.)

Internet Service Provider e-mail

ISPs offer an account where the e-mail can be downloaded on to your own computer. You can therefore access your messages at home, although you will need e-mail software (such as Microsoft Outlook®) in order to read and reply to it. Some ISPs will also provide access to

Table 3.1 E-mail in education

Issue	Advantages	Limitations	Comments
1. Ease	Simple to send a message.	Best for short messages but informal nature of them makes misunderstandings probable.	Most appropriate for asking questions or seeking specific information.
2. Attachments	Documents can be attached to an e-mail. Many types of files can be attached (e.g. documents, video and sound).	Some people will send multiple attachments so you are faced with printing and saving lots of documents. You may have many pages to read and digest.	In order to read an attachment the recipient needs to have the originating application. Some organisations impose a limit on the size of attachments. Sending very large attachments to people accessing the Internet over low speed connections can cause them problems (e.g. long delays while message is downloaded).
3. Non-intrusive	E-mails can be accessed when you are ready for them. They do not intrude as a telephone call may.	It does not allow for interactive conversation but rather a form of discussion similar to passing notes.	
4. Written	E-mail is written and provides you with a record of any discussion.	A series of e-mail messages is difficult to read due to the need to scroll up and down the dialogue.	Informal messages are normal for e-mail but it is easy to misunderstand and in some cases to be offended by them. It is therefore important to be polite. This is often called netiquette.
5. Multiple recipients	Able to send multiple messages with the same effort as a single one.	Often people who are peripheral to the message are copied into the e-mail.	Important to be disciplined in who e-mails are sent to so you avoid wasting their time.

your e-mail online through visiting a website. You need a user name and password but no specialized e-mail application, just a browser. This can prove useful because you can gain access to your e-mail wherever you are: on holiday, at college or using a friend's connection.

Normally web-based e-mail accounts are provided under secure conditions, but in some cases your browser may not allow this and will offer instead an alternative unsecure one. A secure connection employs encryption to stop other people accessing your e-mail and gaining your user name and password. Modern browsers are normally able to support encryption, but if this is not possible you need to decide if you are willing to take the risk. A simple precaution is never to save your password. Many browsers and webpages will ask if you want to save it, meaning you do not have to enter it when you visit again, but this leaves it saved within the browser's records for other people to find.

World Wide Web-based e-mail
There are many providers of free e-mail accounts on the World Wide Web, with which you can send, read and reply to e-mails and add, read and save attachments. However, to take advantage of these services you have to visit the service website and you will need a user name and password. You are always connected to the Internet when using a web-based e-mail, whereas a home ISP account allows you to work on e-mail stored on your home computer without being connected.

College account
Your college will almost certainly provide you with an e-mail account. This allows you to send and receive e-mails from both within and outside the college. You may be able to access your e-mail from external computers. The college account is vital in that your tutors will almost certainly send messages to you through it.

▶ Microsoft Outlook®

Microsoft Outlook® is an integrated e-mail, organizer and diary system. Figure 3.1 illustrates the Outlook 2002 system. It shows that Outlook offers:

- Calendar: essentially a way of planning your appointments so that you can use it to keep track of your course (timetable, lectures, assignments, examinations and any other aspect of your life).

- Contacts: an address book that enables you to keep details of contacts (such as e-mail addresses, websites, telephone numbers and postal address).
- Tasks: allows you to plan your work (such as developing lists of things to do).
- Notes: assists you to make electronic notes so that you do not forget ideas, issues or anything else.
- E-mail: the system provides you with an inbox to hold messages, an outbox to show your replies and new e-mails, plus the functionality to store the messages. You thus have a way of organizing your communications.

It is thus able to provide you with a means of planning, organizing and communicating in relation to your studies. You can:

- produce your own study plan/timetable, breaking down your course into meaningful chunks and identifying priorities
- develop lists of things to do linked to your course
- manage your time so that you meet your deadlines without panic.

The look and feel of Outlook can be changed to meet your preferences.

Customize view
In Figure 3.1 you will see a Customize Outlook Today button with which you can change the way Outlook displays information to you. You can select:

- what folders are presented (on right-hand side of the display you will see that Inbox, Drafts and Outlook have been chosen on this example)
- the number of days of your calendar to show
- to show your task list (that is, today's list or all your tasks)
- the style of presentation (one or two columns).

You need to consider how you prefer to work. This is the initial display, offering an overview of your work. You can see what messages are waiting for you, what your plans for studying are for that day or several days ahead, and a list of the tasks you need to do. It is the equivalent of a notice board where you pin up your course timetable and notes to remind you when assignments are due. However, it offers you the means to organize yourself in depth. It is worthwhile to invest some time in customizing the functions and display to meet your needs. Reflect on your course and needs in order to decide on the customization.

Activity   Outlook

Explore the different ways of customizing Outlook and decide which would be best for you.

Feedback
Figure 3.1 shows one effort to customize Outlook. This person has chosen to:

- add notes to her list of folders since she is quite absent-minded and this will remind her to consider them
- show seven days of her calendar so she can look and plan a week ahead
- show all tasks so she can see everything she is involved with, and set the list to be displayed by due date, so she knows what she needs to do next
- select the Summer style simply because she likes it best: it gives a clear view of everything.

Figure 3.1 A customized Outlook screen

Netiquette

Netiquette is the term given to the rules of conduct you should follow in order to ensure that everyone involved in online communication is treated with respect. Many colleges have developed their own rules of behaviour, and in some cases these have been produced by the students. It is important to check what your college netiquette rules are so that you can follow them.

Activity   Netiquette

Write down a list of rules that you would like everyone to obey when sending e-mails as part of a course.

Feedback
A sample set of rules are:

1. Never use abusive or threatening language.
2. Always write your messages in a polite and friendly manner using the standard forms of start and end (such as 'Dear ...' and 'Best wishes [signature]').
3. Always accept that everyone has a right to an opinion even if it is different from your own.
4. Write in a straightforward informal way so that messages are easy to understand.
5. Check all e-mails with virus protection software to try to remove the possibility of infecting others with a virus.

What were your rules?

▶ Virtual learning environments

Many colleges and universities provide a virtual learning environment (VLE), although these vary considerably in what they offer and even what they are called. They can be called a managed learning environment, a learning platform or simply the intranet. A VLE can offer you:

- access to the library catalogue
- access to course learning materials (such as lecture notes, PowerPoint slides and assignments)
- discussion areas where you can discuss issues with other students

- discussion areas where you can ask questions and tutors will respond to them
- details of your course (such as the assessment approach, timetable and reading lists)
- your records (details of your marks and progress).

The VLE can be used from within the college or accessed from an external site in many cases. Some universities and colleges are now providing information online instead of paper information, so it is important that you become a confident and competent user of the VLE. It is likely that there will be an introductory tutorial available within the environment, so seek it out.

▶ E-mail (sending, forwarding and receiving)

E-mail is now a major way of communicating with your tutors, college administration and other students. It is vital to develop your skills in the effective use of e-mail. These are not simply about technology but also include aspects such as:

- how often you check your messages
- how you write e-mails
- how you respond to messages
- how you organize your messages.

It is good practice to check your messages regularly, and if you have more than one e-mail account it is important to check them all. In some cases you can set an account automatically to forward your mail to another one. This is well worth considering since it will save you time and avoid delays in answering messages. Most e-mail users assume that you will read their messages within a short time of receiving them. If there is a delay they will often become impatient.

Writing e-mail messages
E-mail messages tend to be short and informal, and so they risk being confusing and misunderstood. It is useful to give your messages a consistent structure and to employ plain English so that their meaning is clear. Many e-mails contain mistakes (for example in spelling) which can often cause misunderstandings. It is easy to annoy others with a poor message. This is probably the outcome of a tendency to write

messages quickly and not to check them. It is important to read your e-mails before they are sent and to correct any errors.

Figure 3.2 shows the e-mail message layout in Outlook. Most e-mail systems employ a similar layout, with lines for sender's address, copies and subject. The subject is important since your recipient is likely to see only this listed in his or her inbox along with your name, so you want it to stand out.

On the toolbar above the message area is an Options button. If you select it, a window will appear providing several useful options. These include message settings and receipts.

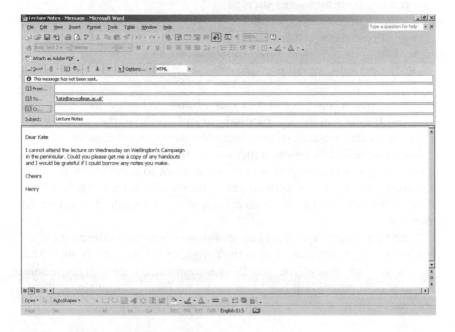

Figure 3.2 Microsoft Outlook® E-mail

Messages can indicate to recipients how important they are (low, normal or high priority) and their degree of sensitivity (normal, personal, or private and confidential). You can also request that a receipt is sent to you when your message arrives or when it is read, although some e-mail systems will automatically block receipts.

You can also specify in the options that any replies to your messages are sent to another address. This is useful if you are sending out a survey and want all the replies sent to another address you have set up, or if you are involved in a group project and one member of the team is coordinating replies.

Responding to messages

All incoming messages are placed in the Outlook inbox. Those that have not been read are shown in bold. The messages can be arranged in several ways. To change the display:

1. Select the View menu.
2. Highlight Current View, to reveal a list of options to help you organize your messages such as:
   • listing messages by sender
   • listing messages by who they were sent to
   • listing messages received in last seven days
   • listing only unread messages.

If you receive a large volume of e-mail and you need to distinguish between the messages, a particularly useful option is the AutoPreview. This shows the contents of the message while in the inbox.

As mentioned earlier, e-mail messages are easy to misunderstand, so if one upsets or angers you, it is important not to reply to it when you are angry. It is best to assume that the message is an error rather than reply in haste and anger. Take your time when responding, and aim for clarity and meaning.

E-mail messages have a major advantage over other communication methods in that they can contain the original message and replies. This allows you to review the whole communication, and is especially useful if communication has been back and forth several times. There are two main approaches to replying. These are:

• Sequential: the correspondents send alternate messages (see Figure 3.3).
• Annotated: a reply annotates the original message. This is used when the original message asks for multiple responses or comments (see Figure 3.4).

A sequential response is normally effective when it is a simple reply, but it can get confusing when the communication has involved several rounds of messages. In order to understand the dialogue, you will sometimes need to read all the messages. It can be useful when

-----Original Message-----
From: Helen
Sent: 04 November 2004 14:58
To: Munira
Subject: Re: Meetings with Alan

Thanks Munira, these are both fine.

-----Original Message-----
From: Munira
Sent: 27 October 2004 12:48
To: Helen
Subject: Re: Meetings with Alan

Hello Helen,
Would Thursday 18th Nov be Ok for you to meet with Alan at 9.00am. He
has appointments from 10am onwards.
Thank you
Munira

-----Original Message-----
From: Helen
Sent: 21 October 2004 15:57
To: Munira
Subject: Meetings with Alan

Hi Munira, could I arrange a series of monthly meetings with Alan please. If
possible I would like to see him quite soon. Just to remind you that
Mondays, Thursdays and Friday mornings are best for me.
Thanks, Helen

Figure 3.3 Sequential reply

replying to summarize all the points. This can avoid confusion and
helps comprehension. If you have copied someone in to an ongoing
dialogue, a summary can be helpful, since a new participant can
sometimes find a long exchange difficult to understand.

When you reply by annotating a message, you need to be careful that
your message is clear. You should be able to see in Figure 3.4 that there
is a danger of the message being misunderstood. In the example, the
reply is shown in bold (on screen it might be in red), but e-mail systems
will often change colours, so even this means of separating out
message and reply is not guaranteed.

**Hi Alan
I have annotated your message below with my response
Cheers
Ian**

Dear Ian
Economics
Please can you let me know which webcasts you would like to take part in. They offer you an opportunity to interact with the specialist tutors who developed the course. The webcasts are produced as an optional part of the programme.
Will there be another opportunity to take part?
The schedule of webcasts is:

Economic Theory, Gordon King, Senior Lecturer; Janet Johnson, moderator
Wednesday, 11 January, 10.00 am – **this clashes with my tutorial which is more important? I would like to take part if I can miss my tutorial.**

Interest Rates **Do you have a description of the content? I am not sure if this is appropriate for me but I could take part.**, Mary Green, Lecturer; Peter Clarke, moderator
Friday, 17 January, 14.30pm

Micro and Macro-economics, Anwar Patel, Lecturer; John Jones, moderator
what is a moderator? I am not sure how webcasts work. Can you explain?
Monday, 23 January, 17.00pm – **I can take part**

European Trade, Jane Drew, Senior Lecturer, Angela Nelson, moderator
Tuesday, 27 January, 16:00pm – **Yes, I can take part in this one**

Many thanks.
Alan

Figure 3.4 Annotated reply

Figure 3.5 shows an alternative to annotation. Nevertheless, you can successfully use annotation if you are careful to make your meaning clear by separating your reply from the original text, using blank lines and avoiding inserting comments in the middle of sentences.

Signature
Most e-mail systems will allow you to add a standard piece of infor- mation at the end of all your messages. This is called a signature. It can

Hi Alan

I can take part in all of the webcasts but I have some questions.

1. Economic Theory, Gordon: this clashes with a tutorial: Is it more important? I would like to take part if I can miss my tutorial.

2. Interest Rates: I am not sure if this is appropriate for me but I could take
part if it is. Do you have the webcast content so I can check if it is suitable
for me?

3. Micro and Macro-economics: I can take part.

4. European Trade: Yes, I can take part in this one.

I am not sure how webcasts work. Can you explain and will there be another
opportunity to take part in the webcast if I am unable to take part this time?
Cheers

Ian

Figure 3.5 Alternative reply

simply be your full name or it can be a longer message. However, it is
added automatically to all your e-mails so it has to be something you
are happy sending to everyone. What is humorous to some people will
almost certainly offend others, so it is worth considering what you
want to say. People add a wide range of messages, such as:

- advertising for a book they have written
- a political or social statement about which they would like to
  influence other people
- a warning that the message is confidential
- postal address and telephone number
- name only.

To create a signature message in Microsoft Outlook®:

1. Select the Tools menu.
2. Choose the Options item to reveal the Options window.
3. Click on the Signature button within the Mail Format tab to
   access the Signature function. When you choose to produce a new

Activity   Reply

Attempt to draft a reply to the message in Figure 3.6 by annotating the original message, but ensure your reply is easy to understand. Your reply needs to say that:

1. The work needs to be shared out among the group.
2. You agree with the summary.
3. You think footnotes are useful.
4. You agree with putting recommendations in order of importance and under the main headings.
5. The photographs will add interest but you did not ask people permission when you took their pictures, and does this matter?

Dear Everyone
I must go out in a minute but I thought it better to send you my ideas for reporting the outcomes of the group project. I thought you might want to consider plans over the weekend. Sorry if my notes are not too clear.

I suggest that:

1. we add a summary to the report
2. we do not use footnotes but include their content in the body of the main report
3. we show the recommendations in order of importance
4. we add the digital pictures that we took to the report: it will improve the report's appearance

It has been suggested by Jane and Briony that we group all the recommendations under the main headings. What do you think?

We need to decide by when we can produce the finished report.

All the best

Peter

Figure 3.6 Message

Feedback
A sample reply is shown in Figure 3.7: as before, the reply is in bold. What do you think? It annotates the original message but adds more blank spaces to separate out the different points, and deletes these parts of the message that are not needed. Would the sender understand the reply?

Activity   Reply – *continued*

Hi Peter

Thank you for your message. I have added my thoughts to your message below but we also need to decide what the role of each member of group should be in writing the final report.

If my comments are not clear please let me know.

Best Wishes

Alan

I suggest that:

1. we add a summary to the report

We need a summary: it will make the report more professional

2. we do not use footnotes but include their content in the body of the main report

I disagree. Footnotes are very useful: why don't you want to use them?

3. we show the recommendations in order of importance

I agree with putting recommendations in order of importance

4. we add the digital pictures that we took to the report: it will improve the report's appearance

The photographs will add interest but I did not ask permission when I took peoples' pictures – I am not sure if that matters

It has been suggested by Jane and Briony that we group all the recommendations under the main headings. What do you think?

I agree with Jane and Briony

Figure 3.7 A reply to the e-mail in Figure 3.6

signature you will be asked to give it a name so you can develop a range to select from. The system allows you to have a different signature for a message you are sending from one that you are replying to or forwarding.

The Mail Format tab also provides access to stationery and fonts (through the Stationery Picker and Fonts buttons, respectively), so you can add a background image on which to write your messages. Again, you need to reflect carefully on how people reading your messages will react to the backgrounds. You can also select the font and character size to use in your messages.

People often receive many e-mails each day. It can be a cause of some concern that a large amounts of time are spent reading and answering e-mail. Your tutors will probably have scores of students, colleagues, friends and family who send them messages. This tends to suggest that short, uncomplicated messages will be appreciated by them, so you need to consider factors such as background, fonts and signature messages. Will they make your messages meaningful, readable and clear, or will they annoy and confuse your readers?

Many people want to convey their personality through the use of backgrounds, fonts and signatures, to make their e-mails distinct so they stand out from the normal pile. This is a legitimate choice, but remember that an e-mail that catches the attention of the reader the first time may irritate when read for the hundredth time.

Spelling

Spelling mistakes are a frequent part of e-mails, but many people will link poor spelling with a casual approach to studying, so you may want to ensure your messages are free of errors. To check the spelling:

1. Select the Tools menu.
2. Choose the Options item to reveal the Options window and the tab called Spelling and Grammar. This offers a range of options to customize checking your messages for spelling errors.

Attachments

One of the most useful features of e-mail is that you can attach a file to the message which will accompany it to your receivers. This lets you submit assignments, share information with other learners in your assignment groups, or even send images home to show your family what your campus looks like. Outlook allows you to add an attachment by clicking on the Paperclip icon in the e-mail compose window, or by selecting the Insert menu and the File option. This opens up the Insert window which enables you to locate the file you want to attach. It is selected by double-clicking on the file, and is then added to your message.

There are several additional factors that you need to consider:

- Some recipients' e-mail systems will not accept attachments.
- Some e-mail systems limit the size of attachments.
- Attachments can contain viruses.
- Recipients can only read the attachment if they have a copy of the application that created it.

You need to check whether people you are sending an attachment to can receive it, and if they have any limits. You will receive an error message if the receiver's system will not accept the message for any reason. Some approaches you can take are:

- If attachments are not accepted, copy and paste information into the main body of the e-mail if this is possible (as it is with, say, a short word processing file).
- If the file is too large you can compress it using an application such as WinZip or break the file down into several smaller files and send them as attachments to several separate e-mails. Alternatively save the files on a floppy disk or CD-Rom and send them by surface post.
- Always check your incoming and outgoing messages with a virus protection application so you safeguard yourself and others from virus attack.
- There are standard file formats that a wide range of applications will read, so it is useful to employ them if you are in doubt. Rich text format (RTF) will be read by most word processors.

E-mail attachments are easy to send, so there is a natural tendency to send messages with more than one attachment. However, reflect on how your recipients will feel if you send 20 attachments, requiring them to print hundreds of pages and spend a long time saving and organizing the files. It is not good practice to save yourself time by passing work on to people who have not volunteered to accept it.

Organizing your messages

The number of e-mail messages that you receive will grow rapidly with your use of the function. It is so straightforward to send a message to a large number of recipients that people use it extensively. It is critical that you are organized to deal with the messages, so that when you want to refer back to an earlier one, you can find it easily. It is frustrating not to be able to locate a message when you know you have saved it. It may be possible to keep your snailmail letters in a box and find one by emptying them on to the floor, but if you adopt a similar approach to e-mail you will waste time, and often not locate the message you need.

Microsoft Outlook® will place all your messages in the inbox folder. You need to create a range of additional folders so that you can separate out the different topics. This will allow you to locate messages efficiently and effectively. To create a new folder from within the inbox:

1. Select the File menu.
2. Highlight the Folders option to reveal a sub-menu of options which includes the New Folder option.
3. Click this option to open the Create New Folder window. Figure 3.8 shows the menus and window.

You can save messages to folders by dragging and dropping them, or by right-clicking on the item and selecting the Move to Folder option. The e-mail can be either read or unread.

So far we have assumed that you want to store your e-mail in folders within the inbox, but you can also save messages to folders in other parts of your system. This can be useful if you want to keep your messages alongside other files relating to the topic. To save to a folder outside the inbox, highlight the message and select the File menu and Save As option.

Rules

You can customize the way that Microsoft Outlook® deals with e-mails using the rules function, which allows you to move different messages into different folders or even to delete them. This is useful if some messages (such as those from your tutor) are more important than others, since it lets you transfer the important messages to a specific folder. Spam or junk e-mail is now a common nuisance to all e-mail users. You can establish rules to filter out spam and therefore not waste your time.

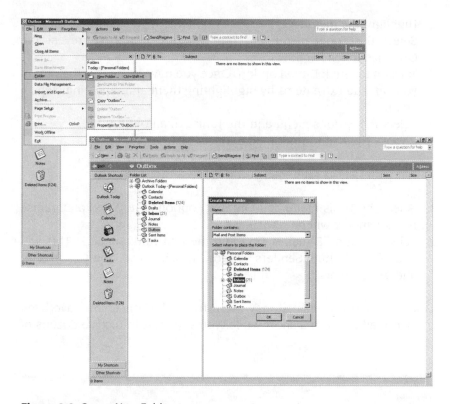

Figure 3.8 Create New Folder

It is important not to answer spam even if it offers you the option to remove yourself from the mailing list, since by replying you confirm that the e-mail address is correct. It thus becomes more valuable to the spammers.

Outlook contains an organize function. To access it:

- Select the Tools menu and choose the Organize option.
- Alternatively, click the Organize button on the Outlook toolbar.

Either action opens the ways to Organize Inbox window (Figure 3.9). This enables you to establish rules to colour-code different types of messages and move different types of messages to specific folders.

In order to add e-mails from a specific sender to the spam/junk mail category:

1. Highlight the message.
2. Select the Tools menu and the Organize option to reveal the Organize Inbox window.
3. Turn on the Junk E-mail option. Once you have turned on the option you can add extra items by highlighting them and repeating steps 4 and 5.
4. Select the Actions menu and the Junk E-mail option.
5. Choose the Add to Junk Mail Senders List.

To edit your lists of junk mail you need to:

1. Select the Tools menu and Organize option. The Ways to Organise Inbox window will be revealed.
2. Select the Junk E-mail option and the Edit Junk Senders. This will open the Edit Junk Senders window, which allows you to add, edit and delete items.

Colour coding your e-mail may seem trivial, but once you have been using e-mail for even a short while, you will start to receive dozens of

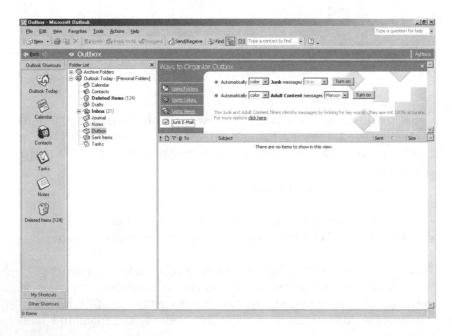

Figure 3.9 Organize window

messages a day. It is important to be able to isolate the important ones at a glance, and colour coding them is very effective.

► Address book

Using Microsoft Outlook® you can create an address book so that you can find people's and organizations' e-mail addresses. This is useful since you will rapidly develop contacts with hundreds of addresses. The address book is accessed by selecting the Tools menu and the option Address Book which, if selected, opens the Address Book window.

You can simply keep a list of e-mail addresses, or use the contacts window to maintain more detailed information about each person such as postal addresses, telephone numbers and other notes about your relationship with that person.

Distribution lists

Outlook offers you the facility to create distribution lists, which are groups of individual addresses under a single name. You can send an e-mail to all the members on the list by using the list name. Distribution lists can be useful within study or assignment groups. The New button provides access to the Distribution List option along with a variety of other useful functions. You can create a list by selecting from the existing address book or by entering new addresses.

Other options

The New button provides access to several other functions such as:

- appointments (to record appointments and, more importantly, to get the system to remind you about them)
- tasks (to plan your tasks)
- notes (to make a note, rather like using a sticky notelet).

These can all be useful when you are studying and need to organize yourself to attend lectures, tutorials or laboratory classes, and contribute to group learning activities, for example. It will also help you if you are combining employment with learning. You can customize the opening display (Figure 3.1) to show you the tasks you need to focus on ,and have reminders appear at intervals to help you achieve your objectives.

▶ Mailgroups

Mailgroups are widely used to encourage discussion, which has always been used in education to encourage learners to contribute to the consideration of a topic and to listen to the views of their peers and tutors. They are simple devices in that by sending an e-mail to a single address, everyone registered with the mailgroup receives the message. Groups vary considerably in size from a single class to possibly thousands of members, although the larger groups are often associated with issues other than formal education such as health, politics or technology. They offer numerous informal learning opportunities.

The purpose of each group is different, but educational mailgroups will often relate to:

• helping you to learn to work in groups, since this is highly regarded in employment
• exploring a specific subject
• learning to listen to other opinions
• making useful contributions
• building on other peoples' ideas
• helping you to reflect on a topic.

Courses often incorporate mailgroups, so it is likely that you will be expected to participate in one or more of them. Some courses assess your participation in online discussions, so that contributions are seen as part of your course. Assessment can take a variety of forms including:

• asking your peers to assess your contributions
• requiring you to incorporate online discussion into assignments
• group assignments.

Many courses require students to work together, mainly face to face, but online discussion can also be helpful. One of the main differences is that while face-to-face discussion is immediate, online allows you more choice of time and place. Another is that a face-to-face discussion normally considers one topic at a time, whereas an online debate will often peruse several different themes in parallel.

You can join in mailgroups as often as you like, but it is probably best to try to participate regularly, since this allows you to follow the contributions to all the different themes. If you only join in occasionally there is a real risk that you will become lost in the range of topic threads.

- Seminar meeting - January 16th   **Joe - 11th November 23.10**
  - re Seminar meeting - January 16th   **Angela - 17th Novemver 11.20**
    - re re Seminar meeting - January 16th   **Fred - 17th November 16.10**
      - re re re Seminar meeting - January 16th   **Sara - 23 November 05.30**
- Assignment   **John - 24th November 10.43**
- Lecture Notes   **Francis - 24th November 17.05**
  - re Lecture Notes   **Jane - 25th November 09.45**
  - re Lecture Notes   **Jane - 25th November 14.32**
    - re re Lecture Notes   **Francis - 26th November 15.03**
- Timetable   **Joe - 27th November 11.12**
  - re Timetable   **Angela - 28th November 00.16**
    - re re Timetable   **Sara - 28th November 11.17**
      - re re re Timetable   **Joe - 29th November 17.18**
      - re re re Timetable   **Fred - 30th November 22.18**

Figure 3.10 Mailgroup discussion

Some mailgroups allow you to track the different themes, but it can be hard work reading through several different streams of discussion in order to participate.

Figure 3.10 illustrates a multiple theme discussion. Mailgroups can present discussions in various ways, and in some cases provide you with choices of presentation. This is simply one option.

Figure 3.10 illustrates the relationship between messages by the indents and the use of the prefix 're'. Mailgroups will often identify who has sent the message and the date and time of sending. The mailgroup provides you with a record of the discussion which you can use as evidence in portfolios or other assessment approaches.

Often mailgroups will be moderated by a member of staff. Moderation is a complex role, a mixture of facilitating the discussion and ensuring that netiquette rules are followed. If the discussion is healthy and vigorous you will probably not see any contribution from the moderator, but if debate is slow, the moderator will often attempt to motivate people to contribute. You can always e-mail the moderator if you need help.

Mailgroups can be used for a variety of types of discussion including an expert seminar or a tutorial. Approaches can differ, but some straightforward ones are:

- Ask an expert on a subject to submit a paper on a particular topic, inviting readers to build on this opening statement. Participants are free to agree, disagree or widen the debate in anyway they feel is appropriate.
- Ask a tutor to provide answers to questions asked online. This is often directly related to the course and is in addition to revision, face-to-face sessions or tutorials.

The expert seminar can last several weeks, with the expert making several contributions and a moderator providing summaries at intervals, whereas the tutorial can be a continuous feature of the course, running in parallel throughout the session.

The earlier section on sending and replying to e-mail messages is very relevant to mailgroups. You want to make contributions that are clear, concise and easily understood, so think through how best to use your e-mails.

Activity   Mailgroups

What are the advantages of an online discussion over a face-to-face one? Write a list.

Feedback
Some of the main advantages are:

1. An online discussion gives participants extra freedom about when they participate. They can choose the time.
2. They can reflect on other people's contributions without the pressure to say something immediately.
3. They can return to an earlier contribution and add an extra comment. People often think of something to say after an interval.
4. They can read all the contributions relating to an issue again, to remind themselves of the points that have already been made.
5. Participants are free to make a contribution at any time. They are not blocked by other participants.

▶ Emoticons

It is difficult to communicate your feeling through e-mail, and it is relatively easy to misunderstand emotions (such as anger). Emoticons, devices that are intended to help people show your emotions onscreen, are small images that you can add to your messages to indicate you are smiling, angry, winking, happy, or whatever. Some people like to use emoticons while others never do. It depends on your own personality and preferences.

If you choose to use them, be confident that your recipients understand the different symbols. If they do not, there is little point in using them. You can locate emoticons by searching the World Wide Web.

Top tips

1. E-mail management systems offer a variety of functions that can help you plan and manage your time, but you must rely on your own discipline in checking them and keeping them up to date.
2. Time spent planning your folder structure for saving your messages will save you many frustrating moments trying to locate them.
3. Never reply in anger to an e-mail message, no matter how provoked you feel. You will often regret it a few minutes later.
4. E-mails are informal communication but remember your purpose is to convey a message, so focus on clarity.

▶ Summary

1.   Customize: select the Customize Outlook Today button.
2.   Options: select the Options button above the e-mail form.
3.   Importance of message: select the Options button and indicate low, normal or high.
4.   Sensitivity of messages: select the Options button and indicate normal, personal, private or confidential.
5.   Receipt: select the Options button and tick receipts box.
6.   Reply: select the Options button and specify that any replies to a message are sent to another address.
7.   Arrange inbox messages: select the View menu and highlight Current View to reveal a list of options.
8.   Signature: select the Tools menu and the Options item to reveal the Options window. The signature function is available within the Mail Format tab by clicking on the Signature button.
9.   Background, fonts and character size: select the Tools menu and the Options item to reveal the Options window. The Mail Format tab provides access to the Stationery Picker and Fonts buttons.
10.   Spellchecker: select the Tools menu then the Options item to reveal the Options window and the tab called Spelling.

11. Attachment: click on the paperclip icon in the E-mail Compose window or select the Insert menu and the File option.

12. New folder: select the File menu and highlight the Folders option to reveal a sub-menu of options which includes the New Folder option.

13. Save messages: drag and drop messages into folders or right click on the message and select the Move to Folder option. To save to a folder outside of the inbox highlight the message and select the File menu and Save As option.

14. Rules: select the Tools menu and the Organize option or click the Organize button on the Outlook toolbar.

15. Add to spam/junk mail: select the Actions menu and Junk E-mail option and choose Add to Junk Mail Senders List.

16. Edit junk mail lists: select the Tools menu and Organize option to reveal the Way to Organize Inbox window, then click on the 'click here' link to open the Edit Junk Senders window.

17. Address book: select the Tools menu and the option Address Book.

18. Distribution lists: select the New button and the Distribution List option.

19. Other options: select the New button and the appointment, task or note option.

4 Finding information (Microsoft® Internet Explorer)

▶ Overview

The skills needed to locate and judge appropriate information are vital in any course. Information comes in many forms. College libraries are a key resource, and many provide computer-based catalogues so that you can quickly locate items. In many cases, catalogues are online, meaning you do not have to visit the library to check the availability of an item. The World Wide Web is an enormous resource with many online journals, collections of research information, online libraries and academic websites.

Finding and using information is a fundamental part of all educational processes. You may be seeking information to help you write an essay, or some research evidence to help you design experiments. In all cases, finding suitable information is central to the task. Information technology now plays a major role in locating, presenting and storing information.

▶ Introduction

This chapter will concentrate on helping you find useful information on the World Wide Web by developing advanced search techniques and quality assurance methods. Most students will have used the Internet, so the emphasis will be on extending your experience.

The chapter will help you to improve:

- searching and navigation
- evaluation of websites
- understanding of e-books
- bookmarking of webpages

- downloading of files
- copying images and information
- the security of your system
- understanding plagiarism
- knowledge of online shopping
- printing.

▶ Browsers

You have almost certainly used a browser to surf the vast collection of websites of the World Wide Web. The most widely used browser is Microsoft® Internet Explorer, which is available in several versions (such as Internet Explorer 6). Microsoft® provides the browser alongside Windows®, and it is fully integrated with Microsoft® Office applications. Nevertheless, there are several others browsers available (including Opera, Mozilla Firefox and Netscape), and these are normally free to download and use. You may wish to explore the different options to determine which browser you prefer.

Once you are connected to the Internet you enter the address (the URL) of the webpage you want to visit, and the browser links you to the site, which is displayed in the browser's main area. You can move backwards and forwards through the webpages by using the forward and back buttons or arrows, depending on the browser being used.

▶ World Wide Web

The World Wide Web is a huge collection of websites containing an enormous amount of information that may be useful to you as part of your studies. By searching the Web you can locate a great deal of useful content. It is rather like having a large library of information in your room. Any individual, organization, government or group can establish a website, so there is a vast variety, covering areas such as:

- Manufacturers of products who provide information about their goods: where to buy them, technical specifications, prices and details of how to contact the company.
- Research organizations: many researchers make their results available online so that you can gain a great deal of information quickly and effectively from a search of the Web.

- Services: train companies, airlines, shipping lines and many other services are available online so that you can buy tickets, check timetables and make sure that services are arriving on time through a visit to the appropriate site.
- Libraries: many universities, colleges and public libraries have made their catalogues available online so you can check that the publication you want is available without visiting the library. Some libraries have publications available in electronic form so you can access a copy from home or college.
- Government bodies: a rich resource of information about government plans, research and resources.
- Electronic journals (e-journals): many research and subject publications are now available online. In some cases you need to subscribe, but you will find that many colleges and universities already do so, meaning you can gain access to the material. You need to check with your library to find out which ones it subscribes to. A wide range of e-journals is also available for free.
- Electronic books (e-books) – many books are now becoming available electronically. They are distributed through online publishers or bookshops. They are often good value, but the range of titles is still limited, although it is expanding. Many e-books require specific reader applications to read them. Two widely used readers are Adobe Acrobat and Microsoft Reader.

The Web does not only contain websites but also offers access to mailgroups and newsgroups.

Mailgroups allow members to send e-mails to a common address, and they are then forwarded to all members. This allows issues to be discussed, ideas explained and questions answered. There are currently thousands of mailgroups, and many colleges and universities now organize mailgroups so that people studying the same subject can easily support each other. Newsgroups are similar to mailgroups, but they are focused on a specific subject. In order to find a group you can use a search engine such as Google (for example, http://groups.google.com/).

▶ Searching and navigating

It is imperative to be able to locate the information you need amongst the millions of websites. After finding the site the next challenge is to decide on the quality of the content, because any person or organization can establish a site, so how do you decide if the information is valid and reliable?

The main way of locating information is via a search engine, which is a website devoted to helping you to find content. They take a variety of forms, but all derive from the concept of a site that indexes the World Wide Web using automatic devices to create a database of webpages. When you use the search engine it finds the desired content in the database and provides you with the URL so you can access the webpage. Search engines locate information by webpage.

Two other types of search engine are also available, directories and meta-engines. A directory is a list of sites where the staff of the search engine have selected specific webpages in response to frequently requested searchers. These are often related to shopping, travel arrangements or similar needs. Many conventional search engines will also offer some form of directory service. Some search engines are essentially just large directories.

A meta-engine searches several different search engine databases simultaneously so that you gain the benefit of effectively searching using different engines. This has the obvious benefit of being thorough and very quick compared to searching them separately.

Whatever type of engine you use, you can search for:

- general information
- images (such as photos)
- news and mailgroups
- news
- shopping
- other specialist services.

Some search engines also offer other services such as:

- e-mail
- help with searching
- translation between languages
- protection from accidentally accessing offensive material.

Website address (URL)

When navigating the World Wide Web, it is important to understand the structure of the address (URL). Like a postal address, it contains useful information. A typical address is: http://www.skills4study.com. This is a website created by Palgrave Macmillan containing free study skills resources. Figure 4.1 shows you the structure of the address.

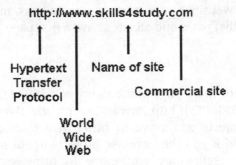

Figure 4.1 Web address

Hypertext transfer protocol is the way that information is moved around the World Wide Web. There are other possible headings such as FTP, which is the file transfer protocol, and indicates a site for downloading files. The name of the site (such as skills4study) sometimes tells you the purpose of the site or the organization that created it. It is often called the *domain*. You can register a domain name, but since many of the common names are now registered, the names of new sites need to be imaginative to reflect their purpose. The final extension (such as .com) indicates that this is a commercial site. There could also be a further extension to show the country of registration (for example, UK indicates United Kingdom). Only sites registered in the United States do not need a country code, but many others do not add a country extension, so it is not a definite indicator of origin.

Some other extensions are:

.co	company or commercial site
.edu	educational organization (college or educational charity)
.ac	academic organizations (such as an university)
.org	charity
.gov	government
.mil	military
.au	Australia
.br	Brazil
.ca	Canada
.eg	Egypt
.gr	Greece
.mt	Malta
.pe	Peru.

Each page of a website has its own unique address, meaning you can directly link to that page, and all sites have a first page called the home page.

Example
The address of the home page of the National Institute for Adult Continuing Education (NIACE) is http://www.niace.org.uk/. If you select the link to research projects you move to http://www.niace.org.uk/projects/Default.htm, and if you then choose projects about information and communication technology you move to http://www.niace.org.uk/Research/ICT/Default.htm. Figure 4.2 illustrates the address of an individual page.

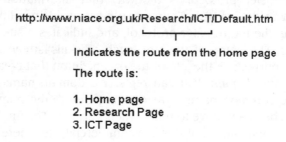

http://www.niace.org.uk/Research/ICT/Default.htm

Indicates the route from the home page

The route is:

1. Home page
2. Research Page
3. ICT Page

Figure 4.2 Individual page address

You can directly access a page if you have its URL. Search engines give you the page addresses for any matches your search makes, so you will go directly to that page.

General searching
Search engines operate by asking users to enter some words relating to the information you are seeking. The engine then provides a list of sites, ranked in order of the engine's assessment of the match between the words and the webpage. In simple terms the engine is matching the words with those on the page. It will often offer thousands, and in some cases millions, of matches.

A search of the World Wide Web using the Google search engine (www.google.co.uk) of the single word 'Chemistry' produced 34,100,000 matches, or *hits*, as they are often called. Limiting the search to the United Kingdom still produced 4,860,000 matches. It is clear that this search term is too wide to be useful. Making the search term 'Organic chemistry' gave 5,270,000 matches, which is better but is still too wide: good searches are normally more specific. A search of 'Organic chemistry tutorials' produced 66,900 hits.

Many users of search engines use very general terms and simply review the top 10 or 20 matches. This may meet their needs, but it does leave the potential of the thousands of other pages unrealized. Obviously it depends on what you are seeking. Some time spent thinking through a good way of describing the information you are seeking may well be rewarded. Good practice is often to enter an obvious set of terms and see what happens. The results give you feedback, and as a result you can improve your search terms.

Activity   Searching

Search for the following key words using two different search engines:

1. Rainfall in Liverpool.
2. Human–computer interaction.
3. Plato.

Feedback
Using Google and MSN gave the following results.
   Rainfall in Liverpool is a fairly precise specification, so there were relatively few hits.

   Google: 29,300
   MSN: 2,648

The top ten matches for both engines had only two in common.
   For human–computer interaction:

   Google: 6,420,000
   MSN: 424,666

The top ten matches for both engines had four in common.
   For Plato:

   Google: 3,810,000
   MSN: 526,683

The top ten matches for both engines had four in common.
   This demonstrates how different search engines have an impact on the matches. It is always good practice to try more than one.
   The World Wide Web is a dynamic environment, so if you repeat this exercise your results will almost certainly be different.

Comparing search engines

Repeating the search series outlined above using the Yahoo! search engine gave the following results:

1. Chemistry: 14,900,000 hits.
2. Organic chemistry: 1,850,000.
3. Organic chemistry tutorials: 38,400.

Using more specific words reduces the number of hits, as the search engine focuses in on your precise needs. A comparison of the top ten matches shows that the two search engines provided five identical matches.

Advanced searching

Most search engines provide you with help to locate information. Among the advanced search techniques are the use of parameters in the search terms such as plus and minus signs, enclosing words in inverted commas, and using Boolean expressions/logical operators (OR, AND and NOT).

The different parameters change the meaning of the search:

- Plus signs: if you link terms with a plus then the search will include only pages where both terms are present. However, some engines will assume a plus sign when you use multiple words.
- Minus signs: if you place a minus sign in front of a word, only matches where the page does not contain the word are included.
- Inverted commas: enclosing a phrase in inverted commas means that matches must contain the whole phrase exactly as presented. Linking the words with plus signs means that matches can be with pages having the words in any order.
- OR: this means that the matches will contain either the first word or the second (for example, Plato OR Socrates).
- AND: this means that both terms linked by AND must be present on matched pages (for example, Plato AND Socrates).
- NOT: this means that matches must contain the first word but *not* the second (for example, Plato NOT Socrates).

You can combine the different parameters and logical operators to produce sophisticated searches.

Example
'Rainfall in Liverpool' matches pages with the whole phrase, and carrying out the search using Google, it produces only two matches. This

indicates the power of these parameters. In this case it suggests that the inverted commas are probably too restrictive. When you search for an exact phrase you need to be sure that all its contents are essential (such as the title of a book, research paper or name of author).

Changing the search to Rainfall+Liverpool produces 29,100 matches, since all pages with both words in any order are present. In Google, simply searching for Rainfall Liverpool without a plus sign gives almost identical results of 29,200 matches. Some search engines assume that when multiple words are given, they must all be present on matches even if you have not used a plus.

Activity   Advanced searches

Using some of the advanced methods, search for webpages covering information on the early military career of Napoleon Bonaparte, Emperor of France.

Feedback
A good start would be to search using Google with the key words 'Napoleon Bonaparte', to investigate the scale of the task. This produces 407,000 hits. Enclosing the name in inverted commas reduces this to 318,000 hits. Adding the phrase 'early military career' and leaving the name enclosed in inverted commas produces 18,700 hits.

At this point it would be sensible to explore the top five hits to see if they provide the right kind of information. The sites are:

1. http://en.wikipedia.org/wiki/Napoleon_Bonaparte
2. http://europeanhistory.about.com/library/readyref/
   blpersonnapoleonbonaparte.htm
3. http://www.carpenoctem.tv/military/napoleon.html
4. http://groups.msn.com/NapoleonBonaparte/books.msnw
5. http://www.napoleonguide.com/leaders_napoleon2.htm

Apart from the first hit, these sites do not focus on Napoleon's early military career, but are more general. However, they do give information about three significant points in his early career:

1. The battle of Toulon.
2. The battle of Lodi.
3. Command of the army of Italy.

A good option at this point would be to search using 'Napoleon Bonaparte' +Army+Italy+Toulon+Lodi. This produces 305 hits.

Sometimes Bonaparte is referred to as simply Napoleon, so it would make sense to consider this possibility. A search based on 'Napoleon Bonaparte' OR Napoleon OR Bonaparte+Army+Italy+Toulon+Lodi produces 551 hits. To add 'military career', since Napoleon was also involved with other issues in this period, cuts this down to 292 hits.

This illustrates the use of advanced search mechanisms. What did you do?

Other search engine services

Search engines may offer the option of advanced searching, which is worth exploring since it will often provide additional facilities. The Google advanced search facility provides you with the opportunity to specify:

- the nature of the key word match (for example, all the words)
- the language of the webpages
- the date the pages were updated
- the file format (for example, pdf acrobat files to locate downloadable resources)
- other refinements.

These can be useful when you are seeking specific information.

Many search engines also have help, preferences and language options which you should explore, since they will assist you to achieve your objectives. The language option within Google provides the opportunity to search for webpages in particular countries, written in a variety of languages, and to translate a webpage or a piece of text.

Google also offers a search directly related to education in Google Scholar, with which you can search for research papers, books and other academic publications. It is available at http://scholar.google.com/. The help system provides useful advice on how to get the best results.

Portals

Another method of locating information is to find a portal relevant to the subject. Those are essentially sites concentrating on providing many links to other sites relevant to the subject. They can be very useful since you are presented with a large number of sources of information.

▶ Evaluating websites

It is difficult to judge accurately the quality of information on a website. It is probably best always to start with the assumption that the information is inaccurate, out of date and poor. In other words you must be persuaded by the evidence that it is correct, suitable and worth using. Anyone can start a website about any topic he or she is interested in, there is no quality assurance mechanism to ensure the accuracy of information on the World Wide Web.

Some ways for validating online information are to:

- Consider who owns the website – is it an appropriate organization, group or individual in relation to the content? A researcher's own website might well provide access to excellent data about his or her work, so do not assume sites run by individuals are always poor.
- Identify when the site content was last updated or enhanced. If the subject is very dynamic (for example, news), the site should be updated regularly. Other subjects however may well need only occasional changes made to them.
- Check the purpose of the site (for example, to sell products). Is the purpose appropriate for what you are searching about? If you want

---

Activity   Evaluate online information

Search for information about the planet Mars. Use the criteria suggested to evaluate the webpages you locate and identify a reliable source.

Feedback
An initial search using the term 'Mars planet' in Google search engine locates 5,530,000 hits, an enormous total. Considering the top five hits:

Hit 1: this references a site sponsored by the US government, which provides access to many high-quality photographic images of Mars and other planets.

Hit 2: this is a wiki, or a website where content can be added and edited by any user.

Hit 3: this is an educational site sponsored by a commercial company.

Hit 4: this is an astrology site owned by an online magazine, with commercial advertising.

Hit 5: this site provides news and references its sources.

All the sites are potentially useful, with the probable exception of hit 4 (unless you are interested in astrology). Hit 1 is a good source of original photographs from space missions, with some useful accurate information from an originating source. Hit 5 provides referenced material which is presented in a concise format for news purposes, but it could be useful for those looking for a summary of the key points. Hit 3 is a potentially motivating and fun site which would be useful if you were seeking material to engage children or adults (perhaps as part of teaching practice or a presentation). Hit 2 is possibly a source of original ideas in that it represents the views of many different people, but it would be potentially difficult to be sure that the content was accurate.
What did you discover?

technical information on a product, then a sales site is probably fine, but in other cases it may not be.

- Check the quality of the content by considering a range of factors such as presentation (including spelling and grammar) and references to other resources.
- Compare information with other sources: is it biased, subjective or flawed?

▶ Bookmarking

Once you have located a useful source of information, the next priority is to ensure that you can find it again. Browsers let you bookmark a webpage so that you can rapidly locate it again. Internet Explorer

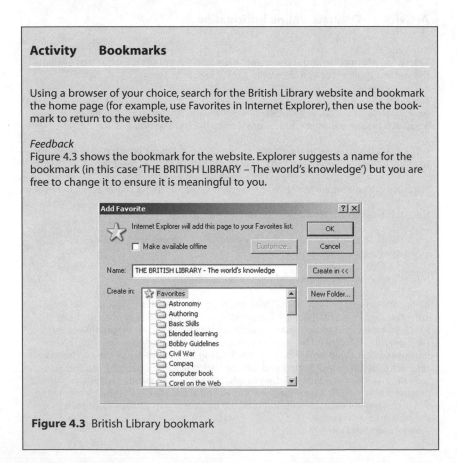

Activity   Bookmarks

Using a browser of your choice, search for the British Library website and bookmark the home page (for example, use Favorites in Internet Explorer), then use the bookmark to return to the website.

Feedback
Figure 4.3 shows the bookmark for the website. Explorer suggests a name for the bookmark (in this case 'THE BRITISH LIBRARY – The world's knowledge') but you are free to change it to ensure it is meaningful to you.

Figure 4.3 British Library bookmark

provides a function called Favorites, which allows you to capture the address of a webpage. To create a favourite (that is, a bookmark):

1. Select the Favorites menu.
2. Choose the Add to Favorites option. When this is selected, the address of the webpage you are viewing will be added to the list within the menu. In order to link to the favourite again you need to select the Favorites menu and click on the name of the page from the displayed list. Within the Favorites menu there is an option called Organize Favorites, with which you can create folders and group your individual bookmarks within them.

▶ Information services

Many websites offer the opportunity to register with them for newsletters or alerts about changes in particular aspects of their contents. This can be useful because it will save you time regularly visiting sites. Several government departments provide regular e-mail newsletters about developments. However, it is easy to find yourself receiving a large number of e-mails from different information sources, and effectively be overcome with too much information.

Google Alerts (http://www.google.co.uk/alerts) is a service provided by the search engine which monitors the web and online news sources for new developments in respect of a particular topic. The service e-mails you to provide the links to the source. You can specify:

- web, news or both to be monitored
- frequency of contact (for example, daily)
- amendments to your request

Other websites such as www.encyclopedia.com offer to locate infor-mation continuously. This is called Topic Tracker, and will provide information relating to a subject. You are again sent an e-mail to make you aware of the new information.

You can track other types of information. For example, real-time train news is available on the National Rail Enquiries site (http://nrekb. nationalrail.co.uk/textme_traintracker/), and you can register to be sent text messages with current train news.

▶ E-books and documents

E-books are electronic books that are produced using word processing applications and then converted into a portable format. There are two major formats, Adobe Acrobat and Microsoft Reader.

E-books can be read on a wide range of products including hand-held devices, Apple Macintosh and personal computers. They are available to buy, and many can also be accessed on the World Wide Web for free. They cover many different subjects, both fact and fiction, and are often available at a lower cost than paper books since they do not have to be printed. They can be read on the screen or you can print them out and read a hard copy.

To access e-books you need the appropriate reader software, and this is freely available. Adobe Acrobat Reader can be downloaded from http://www.adobe.com/products/acrobat/readstep2.html, and Microsoft Reader from http://www.microsoft.com/reader/downloads/pc.asp. Many websites provide electronic documents that you can download, and they also often explain what reader software you need, and how to access it.

▶ Downloading

There are numerous opportunities for downloading files from the World Wide Web, with many sites offering papers, journals and applications. However, you should take great care about downloading anything, since there is always the risk of infecting your system with viruses, spyware or adware. The key steps to take are:

* Decide if you feel the source website is safe: that is, reputable, appropriate and with excellent security.
* Ensure your own virus and spyware protection is operating and will check the files being downloaded.

If you have any doubts, do not download the file.

The second issue is that files are often very large, and if you are connecting to the site through a low-speed connection (for example, a dial-up connection rather than an always-on broadband connection), it can take a long time to download a file. This can be expensive in telephone charges, and there is always the risk that the connection will be broken during the process so you will have to start again. Many sites will tell you the size of the download file, and in some cases, the time to download it over a low speed link.

Some software vendors offer you the opportunity to purchase their product over the Internet, and then download the application so you can start using it immediately. However, the files are sometimes large, so a delay while it is posted to you can be the best choice unless you have a broadband connection.

Some colleges, universities and employers will restrict your rights to download files so as to protect their systems from viruses and spyware. You may find that you can only download to your home computer.

Activity   Downloading a reader application

Select one of the reader applications (such as Adobe Acrobat or Microsoft Reader) and download it onto your computer.

Feedback
For example, you might download the Microsoft Reader if you already have a copy of Adobe Acrobat. In order to download a file from a website, you normally only have to double-click on the file icon. Many sites explain the size of the file. The Microsoft site offers several versions of the application in different languages. It tells you the file is 3.58 Mb and will take 17 minutes to download at a rate of 28.8 Kbytes. This is the slowest speed, and if you are using a broadband connection, it will download considerably quicker.

When you start the downloading process you will see a message appear. The actual message will vary depending on the browser you are using and the type of file you are downloading. All the messages should ask you to decide whether you want to download the file and save it onto your system, to open it in a suitable application (which you might do if it is, for example, a word processor file), or to run it if it is an executable file (a program file ending in .exe). The Microsoft Reader application is an executable file. If it was simply a word processing file, then the message would just offer the choice between saving and opening. In some cases if the file could potentially contain a virus a warning message will be displayed.

If you download an executable file, the browser may well warn that it could contain a virus. If you get this type of message you need to consider whether you trust the source of the file (that is, the website), and to check that your virus protection software is up to date and active. You must judge each case on its merits. The Microsoft site is a reliable source, so if you have good virus protection, you should feel confident in going ahead.

▶ Security

The normal approach to security of college, university or employer systems is to issue users with a user name (sometimes called a user ID) and to ask users to select a password. At regular intervals users are asked to change their passwords so that there is less possibility of other people becoming aware of them. Users are not all given equal rights to the system. Access is graded depending on the degree of security clearance they have. The IT technical staff will have most access, and ordinary users the least. This is essentially based on need. Technical staff need the most freedom since they are required to fix problems, while ordinary users only need access to the 'front end' of the system.

Most users pay little attention to these security measures, but it is important to realize that the only way the system knows who is using it is through the user ID and password. If someone else accesses the system using your ID and password, the system will assume the person is you. This is especially important to bear in mind because in educational systems using virtual learning or managed learning environments, the ID and password could give the user access to personal marks and other assessments. If you allow other people to use your password, they will be able to view your confidential information.

User IDs and passwords are also required when you register for online journals, mailgroups and other services. Many people find remembering different user IDs and passwords difficult, so sites will provide help if you forget your password. Your own computer system can save your passwords so you do not have to remember them. However, a password saved on to a system needs to be protected against unauthorized access in order to secure it.

It is good practice to keep your user ID and password safe and not allow anyone to watch you enter them when you log on to the system. Select a password that it not obvious (for example, use a mix of letters and numbers), and do not keep a written record of your passwords.

▶ Copying images and information

It is often assumed that the information presented on the World Wide Web is free to everyone to use and manipulate as they like. This is not correct. Everything presented on websites is owned by someone, and the degree of free access and use is decided by the owners.

Before copying any website content it is important to find out the conditions that the owners of the material have set. The conditions can vary considerably, from no use beyond the personal use of reading and viewing the site's content on the screen, to complete freedom to amend the content as long as the original source and authors are acknowledged.

The home page is often the best way to find out what the conditions are for using the site's content. They are frequently located at the bottom of the page under links such as 'copyright', 'terms of use' and 'about'. However, the absence of any statement does not mean that you are free to do as you wish. You should assume the opposite – that you cannot use the content except to read and view the material presented.

Activity

Select a range of websites. Identify and compare their conditions for use.

Feedback
Here are some sample conditions:

1. BBC: on the home page at the bottom of the page is a link called 'Terms of Use'. This provides access to a detailed section on the terms under which you can use the content. It restricts use to personal non-commercial use, and forbids actions such as copying.
2. Google UK: on the 'About Google' page is a link called 'Terms of Service' and this again provides detailed guidance and essentially limits users to personal use only.
3. Wikipedia: on the home page is a link called 'Copyrights' which provides access to detailed guidance about the use of the content. You are provided with a license to use the content under the terms of the GNU Free Document License. This lets you copy the content and change it as long as you continue to distribute it under the GNU terms and acknowledge the original authors.
4. Moneymatterstome: in the section about 'Money matters to me' is information about the content, which is provided as a free resource for educational purposes.

These four different sets of conditions illustrate the need to check before you copy or use the content beyond simply reading it on the screen.

▶ Plagiarism

The World Wide Web, along with other sources of electronic documents, is an impressive resource for any student. However, it comes with a significant problem: the danger of plagiarism. If you deliberately or accidentally copy someone else's work it is plagiarism, and all educational institutions regard it as a serious offence. You will certainly fail an assignment if you are discovered to have copied, and you may even fail the course.

It is a normal part of academic study to quote from research or evidence, but this must be acknowledged with a reference to your source. If you do not do this, it can be considered as plagiarism. Many students find it confusing that you can quote as long as you acknowledge the source through a reference, but you cannot copy. The difference is the acknowledgement and the length of the quote. Normally you are only quoting a short segment (a phrase, sentence or brief section) and are integrating the quote within your own work so that it aids your argument or reasoning. You are not stealing the concept, idea and words by pretending they are your own work. Your college will be able to provide you with guidance about plagiarism.

Your own college or university will have guidelines about how to cite a source on the World Wide Web, but the reference is normally the URL, the title and name of author of the document, if they are given, and the date the webpage was accessed. The latter is important since websites are dynamic and liable to change.

There are now several electronic checkers that can read an assignment and check it against documents published online, so it is now becoming relatively easy to check for plagiarism involving the World Wide Web.

Activity   Plagiarism

Search the World Wide Web for 'plagiarism' and see what you can learn about the subject.

Feedback
A straightforward option is to use Google.co.uk and search simply using the word 'plagiarism'. This produced 2,530,000 hits. On the first page of the search there were eight sites specializing in identifying plagiarism, and five aimed at helping people to avoid accidental plagiarism. The emphasis in the information on several of the sites is that you should provide references for any material you quote, use your own words and ideas, and if you paraphrase, do not follow the original source too closely. Essentially, be original, use your own words and ideas, limit the number of quotes, give full references for those you do use, and don't copy.

▶ Online shopping

The World Wide Web offers a variety of opportunities to buy books and computer applications that can aid your studies. Several online bookshops offer enormous ranges of titles, so you should be able to locate any books you need for your course. There are also many opportunities to buy second-hand, out-of-print and other scarce titles.

Activity   Second-hand books

Search the World Wide Web for websites selling second-hand books. What can you find?

Feedback
Using Google.co.uk and searching simply using the phrase 'second-hand books for sale' produced 5,180,000 hits. The first was abebooks.com, which is a site many academics use to find out-of-print and second-hand books. It claims to be the largest online marketplace for books, and offers a search facility to locate the publication you are seeking. The home page provides a special function to find text books for learners.

▶ Printing

You can print webpages using the print option with the File menu in Internet Explorer. However, it is worth remembering that a webpage is often a great deal longer than a conventional page, so that rather than getting a single page of printout, you might end up printing many sheets. If you only want a small element this can be very wasteful. Webpages are sometimes wider than a printed page, so you will find your printouts may miss the right-hand edge of the content.

It is therefore important to use Print Preview to check what you are printing (select the File menu and Print Preview option) and use Page Setup to change to landscape, adjust scales or change margins so the whole page will appear on the printout (select the File menu and Page Setup options). Once you have checked and adjusted your printout you can print the webpage by selecting the File menu and Print option.

Top tips

1. **Searching:** the World Wide Web is a major resource but unless you can locate the information, it is of little use. A systematic approach will bring benefits.
2. **Judging sites:** anyone can set up a website, so consider the quality of the information presented. Look at who owns the site, when was it last updated, and check whether the information is supported by other sources.
3. **Security:** viruses, adware and spyware can make your life miserable, so take precautions to stop them infecting your system.
4. **Plagiarism:** don't do it.

▶ **Summary**

1.   To access a website: enter the website address (URL) into the browser's address.
2.   Navigation (forward and backwards): click on the forward or back buttons.
3.   Search: enter keywords into the search engine.
4.   Advanced search: use parameters in the search terms such as plus and minus signs, enclosing words in inverted commas and using Boolean expressions/logical operators (OR, AND and NOT).
5.   Other search engine services: the Advanced Search option often provides extra facilities such as the nature of the key word match, the language of the webpages, the date pages were updated, and file format.
6.   Bookmarks: locate the webpage and select the Favorites menu then the Add to Favorites option.
7.   Organize bookmarks: select the Favorites menu and the Organize Favorites option.
8.   Download: double-click on the file and select whether to open, save or run it.
9.   Copyright: explore the home page for links such as 'copyright', 'terms of use' and 'about'.
10.   Page setup: select the File menu and the Page Setup option.
11.   Print preview: select the File menu and the Print Preview option.
12.   Printing: select the File menu and the Print option.

5 Organizing information (Microsoft® Access)

▶ Overview

Once you have found or created information and resources the next step is to ensure that you can locate it again weeks or even months later. A brilliant resource is no use if you cannot remember where you found it when you need to include it in your dissertation or list it in your references. A detailed set of notes is only helpful if you have ready access to them. There are many ways of organizing your information, for example establishing a filing system, but you will find that a database gives you the extra benefits of comparing and contrasting your resources, adjusting their presentation, and printing out their contents in many different ways.

▶ Introduction

This chapter will assist you to organize your information through developing and using databases. You may have some experience of using databases such as library catalogues, but you have probably never constructed one, so this chapter will focus on developing databases for your own use. It does assume you are a confident computer user and comfortable with using Microsoft Windows® and Microsoft® Office applications.

The chapter will be based around Microsoft® Access 2002, and will cover:

- creating a database table
- searching database tables
- formatting and presenting reports
- querying the information stored in a database table
- relational databases.

Microsoft® Access is available in a variety of versions:

- Access 95
- Access 97
- Access 2000
- Access 2002.

You may be using any of these versions, since they represent the development of the product over the past nine years. People often purchase Microsoft® Office, which is an integrated range of products (word processing, spreadsheets, databases and so on). Microsoft® Office is again available in a range of versions (such as Office 95, Office 97, Office 2000 and Office 2002), which align with the version of the individual products. The techniques described in this chapter are based on Access 2002. However, you should be able to transfer them to any version of Access to which you have access, and we provide you with hints and tips to make this easier.

▶ Creating a new database

With many computer applications it is reasonable to adopt the approach of experimenting and exploring the possibilities. However, to develop a database requires careful preparation. Access allows you to create a database rapidly, but it may well be poorly structured if you do not consider what you are trying to achieve.

During this chapter we shall concentrate on illustrating the development of a reference database to store details of books, papers and websites that you have located during your studies. This is a useful database for almost any course, since it is a common problem to lose track of the source of information. It is often a time-consuming task trying to find the full reference for an author you wish to quote in an essay or other form of assignment. During revision you will often want to locate useful sources quickly, and a database will help you to do this.

In order to create a database you need to understand three information items. They are:

- field
- record
- table.

A *field* is a single item of information (such as a street name), while a *record* is a collection of fields relating to a common topic (such as the address of a building – street, town and postcode). A *table* is a series of records (such as addresses of a group of friends).

In the database we are aiming to create we shall include the following information:

- books: author, publisher, ISBN number and date of publication
- papers: author, journal title, page references, publisher and date of publication
- websites: URL, author and date of access.

When creating a database you need to decide what type of information each item comprises (for example, a number). This allows the database to sort the information, and allow sufficient memory space to store the item and manipulate the information (such as undertake calculations on numerical information). Microsoft® Access has defined nine types of information. They are:

- Text: up to 255 letters and numbers (collectively known as characters).
- Memo: up to 64,000 letters and numbers. This allows you to store a chunk of text such as a comment on a book or paper.
- Numbers: a range of different types of number (for example whole numbers or integers).
- Date and time.
- Currency (money).
- Autonumber: Access automatically produces a new number so that individual items can be given a unique number.
- Yes/no: the data can only consist of one of two alternative items, such as good or bad.
- OLE Object: data from other Office applications such as word processing files, pictures and so on.
- Hyperlink: links to websites.

Table 5.1 shows the different data types assigned to the information in our sample database. You will notice that the author item has become two fields for first and last names, and we have also added a comment field. This enables you to explain the contents and usefulness of the source for when you are considering it some time later. The item number will allow each book, paper and website to be individually numbered. The number of characters for a text field is based on the length of typical

Table 5.1 Data types

Table	Field name	Data type
Books	Item Number	Autonumber
Books	Title	Text – 50 characters
Books	First Name	Text – 25 characters
Books	Last Name	Text – 25 characters
Books	Publisher	Text – 35 characters
Books	ISBN number	Text – 25 characters
Books	Date of Publication	Number
Books	Place of publication	Text – 25 characters
Books	Comments	Memo
Paper	Item Number	Autonumber
Paper	Title	Text – 50 characters
Paper	First Name	Text – 25 characters
Paper	Last Name	Text – 25 characters
Paper	Journal Title	Text – 35 characters
Paper	Page	Number
Paper	Publisher	Text – 35 characters
Paper	Date of Publication	Date and time
Paper	Comments	Memo
Website	Item Number	Autonumber
Website	URL	Text – 60 characters
Website	Title	Text – 50 characters
Website	First Name	Text – 25 characters
Website	Last Name	Text – 25 characters
Website	Date	Date and time
Website	Comments	Memo

words that will form the field. In this case most last names are no longer than 25 characters, so this is a sensible length to choose.

▶ Microsoft® Access: create a new database

This section is best read with the Access application on the screen in front of you. Microsoft® Access is an application designed to help you create databases. To start the process of creating a new database, you need to:

1. Select the Blank Database option in the New File display on the right side of the display (in Microsoft® Access 2002). If this is not visible then select the File menu and the New option which will open the right-side display.

2. This will open the File New Database window so you can save the new blank database in a folder of your choice with a meaningful name.
3. In this case we have selected the name 'References.mdb'. The file extension indicates it is an Access database.

The process is the same for creating a blank database in earlier versions of Microsoft® Access except that the option Blank Database is displayed in a window rather than on the right-hand side of the Access screen when the application is initially opened.

Once you have saved the file, the References window shown in Figure 5.1 is opened, enabling you to create tables of information and enter data into them. In our project we have three tables to construct for books, papers and websites. You are provided with two approaches to creating tables, Design view or using a wizard. The wizard is intended to help you construct a table by choosing from options, and is generally intended for those users with less experience. However, Design view provides an opportunity to see how a database is constructed, and may help you understand the workings of other databases that you need to use. We shall therefore employ Design view. Again earlier versions (such as Access 97) have a similar process, but the References Database window is presented in a different way.

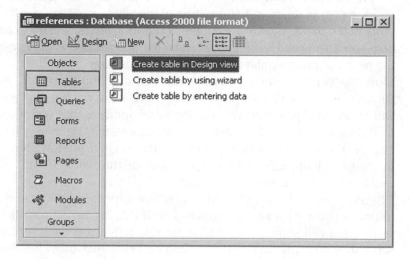

Figure 5.1 References Database

The options down the left-hand side of the window are offered as a series of tabs across the top of the window. Once you have selected a tab, you then pick the Ncw button to open a second window with the options to choose Design view or the Table Wizard.

Creating a table in Design view

To create a table:

1. Select Create Table in Design View. The new window shown in Figure 5.2 is opened. This allows you to enter the various fields and their respective data types. Figure 5.3 shows the information that needs to be entered for books.
2. Enter the information by clicking in the field name box and using the keyboard to enter text.
3. Enter the data type box by clicking in the box to reveal a button with a down arrow. If this is clicked, then a list of the data types is revealed and you can select a type by clicking.
4. Once you have selected a data type you will see that at the bottom of the window, in the General tab, a sequence of extra sections will appear. These let you adjust details of the data type such as length of text.
5. Adjust the type by clicking in the box and amending the default value (for example, 50). You can also click in the box to reveal another down arrow button. You adjust the data type by clicking on the button to reveal a list of options from which you select. You will notice that notes appear in the right bottom area of the window to help you.
6. Write notes about your choices in the description boxes, and they can help you if you need to edit your fields. In earlier versions of Access the process is very similar and the windows are almost identical.
7. Close the window when you have finished entering the fields, by clicking on the close button in the top right-hand corner, and you will be asked if you want to save the table. Indicate that you want to do so, and you will be asked to enter a name. Here we shall choose 'Books'. The window closes and the original window shown in Figure 5.1 appears, with the addition of the word 'Books' to indicate you have created a new table.
8. Observe a warning message (this may not appear in some cases) asking if you want to set a primary key. If this happens then click on No. You will sometimes need to be able to identify each record separately. The primary key is a field or fields that provides this identification.

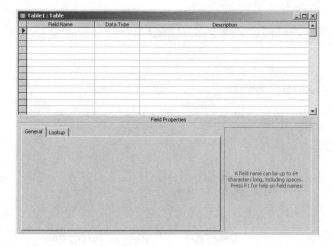

Figure 5.2 Table creation in Design view

Field Name	Data Type	Description
Item number	Autonumber	
Title	Text	50 characters
First Name	Text	25 characters
Last name	Text	25 characters
Publisher	Text	35 characters
ISBN number	Text	25 characters
Date of Publication	Number	Long integer – year
Place of Publication	Text	25 characters
Comments	Memo	

Figure 5.3 Completed table

Activity   Create a table

Attempt to produce the Books table following the instructions given, and if you feel confident, create the Paper and Website tables. Remember you need to open a blank database as the first step.

The Paper and Website tables are shown in Figures 5.4 and 5.5 below:

Feedback
How did you do?

You should now have a References window (Figures 5.1 and 5.6) with Books, Papers and Websites tables listed. It will now read: ▶

Activity   Create a table – *continued*

Create Table in Design View
CreateTable by using Wizard
Create Table by Entering Data
Books
Papers
Websites

You can open the tables by clicking on them. If you are using an earlier version of Access the tables will still appear in the references database window.

Field Name	Data Type	Description
Item number	Autonumber	
Title	Text	50 characters
First Name	Text	25 characters
Last name	Text	25 characters
Journal Title	Text	35 characters
Page	Text	Long integer
Publisher	Text	25 characters
Date of Publication	Date/Time	Short Date e.g. 12/12/2005
Comments	Memo	

Figure 5.4 Paper table

Field Name	Data Type	Description
Item number	Autonumber	
URL	Text	60 characters
Title	Text	50 characters
First Name	Text	25 characters
Last name	Text	25 characters
Date	Date/Time	Short Date e.g. 20/08/2005
Comments	Memo	

Figure 5.5 Websites

Using the wizard

If you are not confident that you can create a table using Design view, the alternative is to employ the Create Table by using Wizard option, which allows you to produce a table by choosing from options. Figure 5.6 shows the Table Wizard. To create a table using the wizard:

1. Select Create Table by using Wizard.
2. Select the Personal options by clicking on the Personal radio button and Books table from the list; you will see the sample fields change (Figure 5.6).
3. Choose the fields by clicking once on the item and then the single arrow button. The field will now appear in the final window – Fields in the new table. The Table Wizard works in the same way in earlier versions of Access but the window is presented in a slightly different way, so you will need to seek the options which appear in different parts of the display.

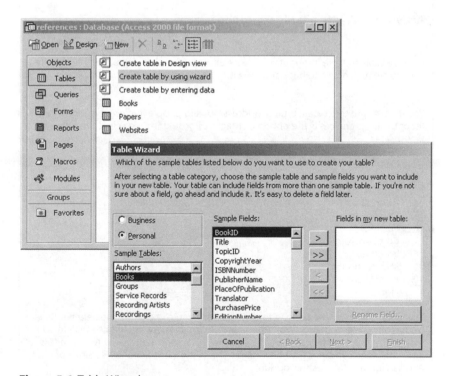

Figure 5.6 Table Wizard

Choose the following fields:

- Book ID
- Title
- PublisherName
- Copyrightyear
- PlaceofPublication
- Notes

4. Click on the Next button once you have added all your fields, and the new table will appear in the Reference window. You will be asked to name the table. Call it 'Books Wizard'.

You will have noticed that the fields are not identical to the table we designed. This is the main limitation of the wizard system. You are restricted to the available choices. It is however possible to change and amend your choices. In order to edit the fields (including adding extra ones):

Activity   Create a table using the wizard

Create a table to store information of your choice using the wizard. You will initially have to create a new database and save it.

Feedback
You might want to create a type of address book of people and organizations. In the list of business choices is the option Contacts. Choose this then select the following fields:

1. ContactID
2. FirstName
3. LastName
4. Address
5. City
6. PostalCode
7. CompanyName
8. WorkPhone
9. MobilePhone
10. EmailName
11. Notes.

There is a button on the table wizard with which you can change the field name. You might use it to change WorkPhone into Telephone. You highlight the field you wish to rename and then click on the button. This opens the rename field window into which you can enter your new name. This is the same in earlier versions of Access. Figure 5.7 shows this option.

1. Highlight the table Books Wizard.
2. Select the Design option on the toolbar. This will open your table in Design view (Figure 5.2) showing the fields you have previously selected so you can add, remove and edit fields. Enter two new rows into Design view to create two new fields, First Name (text – 25 characters) and Last Name (text – 25 characters). Again the process is the same in earlier versions of Access but the options are presented in different places. You now have a Books table that has the same fields as the one created using Create Table in Design View.

Enter data

The next step is to enter data into the three tables, since so far we have only created blank templates for the information. We will concentrate on the Books table since this will allow you to use either version, the one created in Design view or the one created using the wizard. Table 5.2 provides some information to enter into the table.

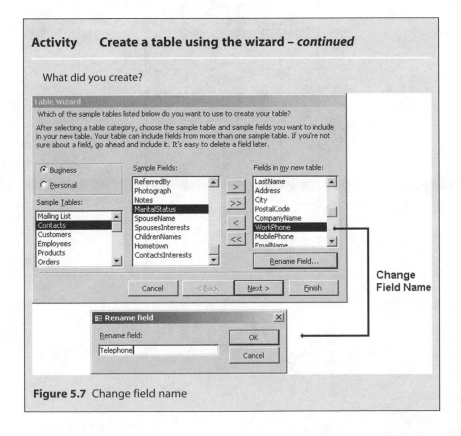

Activity   **Create a table using the wizard – *continued***

What did you create?

Figure 5.7 Change field name

Table 5.2 Book table information

Item number	Title	First name	Last name	Publisher	ISBN	Date of publication	Place of publication
1	e-Learning Skills	Alan	Clarke	Palgrave Macmillan	01403917558	2004	Basingstoke
2	The Futurians	Damon	Knight	John Day	0381982882	1977	New York
3	Evaluating Training Programs	Donald	Kirkpatrick	Berrett-Koehler	01576750426	1998	San Francisco
4	Digital Photography	Peter	Bargh	Hodder and Stoughton	0340867493	2003	London

Activity   Data entry

Insert the four records from Table 5.2 into the Books table, then add the extra four below:

Online Education, Greg Kearsley, Wadsworth, 0534506895, 2000, Belmont

Gettysburg, Hugh Bicheno, Cassell, 0304356980, 2001, London

General Lee, Walter Taylor, University of Nebraska Press, 0803294255, 1994, Lincoln

With Pen and Saber, Robert Trout, Stackpole Books, 0811719308, 1995, Mechanicsburg

The width of the columns can be adjusted in the same way as you alter Excel spreadsheet columns, by placing the mouse pointer over the column title bar line. The pointer changes shape to form a double arrow and allows you to drag the column border and change the width. Adjust your columns so that the information can be viewed.

Feedback
Figure 5.8 shows the process of dragging the column to adjust the width to display the full title of the book, while Figure 5.9 shows the table with all records entered.

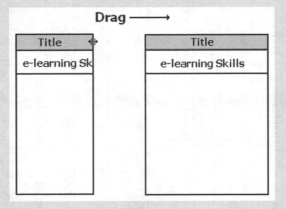

Figure 5.8 Extra records

Activity   Data entry – continued

Item number	Title	First Name	Last Name	Publisher	ISBN number	Date of publication	Place of publication
1	e-Learning Skills	Alan	Clarke	Palgrave Macmillan	01403917558	2004	Basingstoke
2	The Futurians	Damon	Knight	John Day	0381982882	1977	New York
3	Evaluating Training Programs	Donald	Kirkpatrick	Berrett-Koehler	0157675042 6	1998	San Francisco
4	Digital Photography	Peter	Bargh	Hodder and Stoughton	0340867493	2003	London
5	Online Education	Greg	Kearsley	Wadsworth	0534506895	2000	Belmont
6	Gettysburg	Hugh	Bicheno	Cassell	0304356980	2001	London
7	General Lee	Walter Taylor	Taylor	University of Nebraska Press	0803294255	1994	Lincoln
8	With Pen and Saber	Robert	Trout	Stackpole Books	0811719308	1995	Mechanicsburg

Figure 5.9 Books table

To enter information into the tables we have created:

1. Double click on the table name, and the Books table will open so you can type in your data.
2. Enter your data. Table 5.2 shows the four records that you need to enter for the Books table. As you enter them into the Books table, each row is created automatically as you fill the records, and the item number is filled in by the system. The process is identical in different versions of Access.

▶ Editing

A key factor with any database is careful planning to design the correct tables, but there will be occasions when you want to edit the data or alter the structure. Access provides functions to help you do this. The main editing approaches are:

- Simply clicking into a field will allow you to add, delete or change the information it contains.
- The Edit menu offers you functions to:
  1. Delete Column.
  2. Select Record (that is, highlight it) in order to operate on it (for example, delete it).
  3. Select All Records (that is, highlight all of them) in order to operate on them (for example delete them).
- The Format menu functions may require the column or record to be highlighted (selected) before they can operate. The menu has functions to alter:
  1. Font (to change the font, font style and character size).
  2. Datasheet (to alter the formatting on the data sheet – background colour, gridline colour, cell effects, showing vertical/ horizontal lines and appearance of table borders).
  3. Row Heights.
  4. Column Widths.
  5. Rename Column.
- The Insert menu lets you add a:
  1. New record.
  2. Column (that is, a new column inserted to the left of the cursor position).

You should take great care when editing your records, since changes are usually permanent and you cannot use 'Undo' to change your mind. The editing process is broadly similar in earlier versions of Access.

Activity   Editing

Edit the Books table to improve its appearance. You are free to make any changes that you feel are appropriate.

Feedback
Let's take as an example some quite simple editing. Use the Format menu option Font to change it to Tahoma, emboldened with a character size of 10. Changed the row height to 16 and then used the Format menu Datasheet option to select the raised cell effect. Figure 5.10 shows the results of these changes.

Item number	Title	First Name	Last Name	Publisher	ISBN number	Date	Place of Publication	Comments
1	e-Learning Skills	Alan	Clarke	Palgrave Macmillan	0140391755	2004	Basingstoke	
2	The Futurians	Damon	Knight	John Day	0381982882	1977	New York	
3	Evaluating Training Program	Donald	Kirkpatrick	Berrett-Koehler	0157675042	1998	San Francisco	
4	Digital Photography	Peter	Bargh	Hodder and Stought	0340867493	2003	London	
5	Online Education	Greg	Kearsley	Wadsworth	0534506895	2000	Belmont	
6	Gettysburg	Hugh	Bicheno	Cassell	0304356980	2001	London	
7	General Lee	Walter	Taylor	University of Nebras	0803294255	1994	Lincoln	
8	With Pen and Saber	Robert	Trout	Stackpole Books	0811719308	1995	Mechanicsburg	
(AutoNumber)						0		

Record: 1 of 8

Figure 5.10 More formatting

► Searching databases

Entering information into a database table is obviously important, but the main point is to find the information again when you need it. Access provides several functions to help you locate information, or to view the table in ways that help you find what you are seeking. Some useful functions are:

- Sort Ascending
- Sort Descending
- Find
- Go To
- Filter
- Query.

Sorting in a table is often very effective when you are trying to see the pattern within the information. It will help you browse the data to locate what you are seeking or provide a systematic presentation. Access provides two ways of sorting data in a column, either ascending or descending. Ascending means into order of the lowest to the highest number, or alphabetically from A to Z. Figure 5.11 illustrates this type of sort.

Alphabetical order	Lowest to highest
Digital Photography	1977
e-Learning Skills	1994
Evaluating Training Programs	1995
General Lee	1998
Gettysburg	2000
Online Education	2001
The Futurians	2003
With Pen and Saber	2004

Figure 5.11 Sorting ascending

Descending means sorted into order of the highest to the lowest number or reverse alphabetical (Z to A). Figure 5.12 illustrates this type of sort. In order to sort information, you need to click in the column and then select the Sort Ascending or Descending icon on the table datasheet toolbar. The sort icons are the same as those in Microsoft® Excel. These options are available in earlier versions of Access.

Reverse alphabetical order	Highest to lowest
With Pen and Saber	2004
The Futurians	2003
Online Education	2001
Gettysburg	2000
General Lee	1998
Evaluating Training Programs	1995
e-Learning Skills	1994
Digital Photography	1977

Figure 5.12 Sorting descending

Sorting is clearly a useful way of dealing with your information, but if you simply want to locate a specific item, it is not the most effective. Access offers two different approaches to finding information directly. The first is:

1. Select the Edit menu and the option Find. A window entitled Find and Replace appears, with which you locate a particular word or phrase in the table of your choice.
2. Enter the word or phrase you are seeking. When the word is located, it is highlighted.

The Find and Replace window enables you to change the found word or phrase with another, using the Replace tab. This can be useful way of editing your information, especially if you are seeking to change a word that appears several times in the table. The window provides options for you to select the way Find works (such as where to look for the match, to match with whole field or part of it, and to match the case).

The second alternative is:

1. Select the Edit menu.
2. Highlight the option Go To, to reveal the choices. This is a more limited function than Find.
3. Choose an option to move to different parts of the tables. This is useful when the table becomes large. The different options are go to:
   • First: first record in table.
   • Last: last record in table.
   • Next: next record in table.
   • Previous: previous record.
   • New record: the empty bottom line which is ready for an additional record to be entered.

The Datasheet toolbar provides three icons relating to the filter function. If you position your pointer over the icons, their names will appear. These filters are available in earlier versions of Access. Filters allow you to display only selected records. The three filter icons are:

   • Filter by Selection.
   • Filter by Form.
   • Apply Filter.

To filter by selection:

1. Highlight a specific field and select the Filter by Selection icon. The filter will display records that match the contents of the field.

Example
Highlight London in the Place of Publication field and click on the Filter by Selection icon. Figure 5.13 shows the display.
2. Add extra items by repeating the process of highlighting and filtering in the filtered display.

Item number	Title	First Name	Last Name	Publisher	ISBN number	Date of Publication	Place of Publication	Comments
6	Gettysburg	Hugh	Bicheno	Cassell	030456980	2001	London	
4	Digital Photography	Peter	Bargh	Hodder and Stoughton	0340867493	2003	London	

Figure 5.13 Filter by selection

3. Close the window and you will be prompted to save changes.
4. Save your filter, by accepting the offer.
5. Show the filtered display by selecting the third icon – Apply Filter.
6. Remove the filter by right clicking on the filtered display and select the <u>R</u>emove/Sort option.

Filter by form is another way of filtering the records, but it is unlikely to be useful with databases you have created for your own use.

Queries
Access provides the means to ask questions of the information that you have stored in your database. This can be useful because you can query information stored in one or many tables. Queries can take several forms. These are:

- Select: takes information from one or more tables and displays it.
- Total: undertakes mathematical operations (such as sum).
- Action: these allow you to alter your information (such as update the information).
- Crosstab: lets you show information in a form similar to a spreadsheet.

- SQL (Structured Query Language): this is designed to be used in advanced databases.

We shall concentrate on the Select type since this is the most appropriate for databases designed to help an individual keep records. To create a query:

1. Select the Query option in the database (references) window (Figure 5.1). This changes the window display to show two options:
   - Create Query in Design View.
   - Create Query by using Wizard.
2. Click the New button, and the New Query window opens (Figure 5.14).
3. Select one of the new query types from this window, or click on either of the two options in the database window. The wizard allows you to create a query by selecting from options, while Design view requires a little more confidence and understanding. We shall use Design view, since the structure of a query will be demonstrated. However, if you are simply aiming to display a selection of informa-

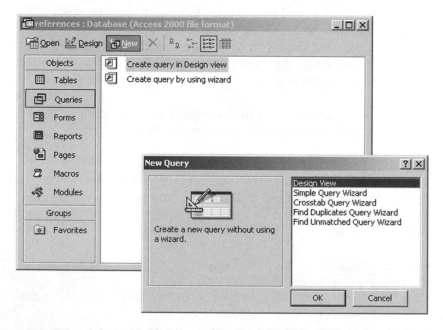

Figure 5.14 New query window

tion from your table, the wizard provides a quick and efficient way of doing this.

4. Select Create Query in Design View, and two windows will appear as shown in Figure 5.15. The same display is shown in earlier versions of the application (such as Access 97). The smaller window displayed on top is called Show Table and the lower window is called Query1: Select Query. Show table allows you to select the tables you want to query. In this case the choice is:

- Books
- Books Wizard
- Papers
- Websites.

There are two other tabs which show you queries you have created and saved, and a joint list of queries and tables.

5. Select tables for your query by highlighting them and clicking on the Add button. Select Books. Your selected table will appear in the lower window.

6. Click the Close button when you have finished in order to remove the Show Table window. You will be left with the lower table now holding the Books table. It is possible to design a query to question more than one table, but the main benefit is that the tables contain information that is related. In the section 'Relational databases' (pages 142–4) this will be explained in more depth. Figure 5.16 shows the process of selecting the fields to display when the query is run.

7. Click in the Field row in the first column and a down arrow button will appear.

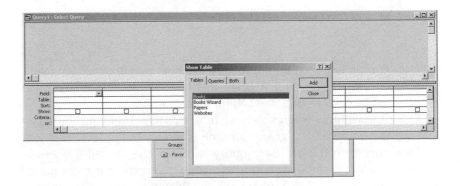

Figure 5.15 Select query window

8. Click on the down button to reveal a list of the Books table fields (Figure 5.16). A field is chosen by clicking on one of the listed fields. In the Table row the Books name is inserted automatically. In the third row another down arrow button appears, giving you three choices for sorting the information: ascending, descending and not sorted. The fourth row provides a tick box so that you can select to display the information in the field. The fifth and sixth rows allow you to add special criteria.

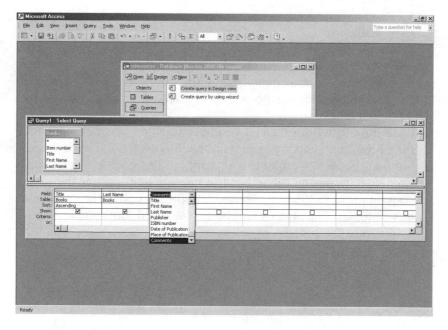

Figure 5.16 Selecting fields

9. After completing a column, move to the next one in order to repeat the process of selecting a field. In the example shown we have selected to display Title, Last Name and Comments.

10. Close the window when you have finished. You will be prompted to save the query and to give it a name (such as Example1). This will then appear in the database query window. The overall process is very similar in earlier versions of Access. To display the results of the query you need to double-click the Example1 item. The result is shown in Figure 5.17.

Title	Last Name	Comments
Digital Photography	Bargh	
e-Learning Skills	Clarke	
Evaluating Training Programs	Kirkpatrick	
General Lee	Taylor	
Gettysburg	Bicheno	
Online Education	Kearsley	
The Futurians	Knight	
With Pen and Saber	Trout	

Figure 5.17 Results of query

▶ Printing

You can print your records by selecting the File menu and Print option to reveal the Print window. This provides three options:

- All: the whole table.
- Pages: specific pages.
- Selected Record(s): specifically highlighted records.

▶ Reporting

Access enables you to create different presentations of selected table information. These are called reports, and can contain any combination of information. You can save several different reports so you have standard ways of presenting information. To create a report:

1. Select the Reports option in the Database (References) window (Figure 5.1). This changes the window display to show two options:
   - Create Report in Design View.
   - Create Report by using Wizard.
2. Select Create Report by using Wizard. The Report Wizard window allows you to select which table or query to create a report for.
3. Select a table or query, then choose which fields to include in the report.
4. Select the fields and click on the Next button to reveal the option to group information. Again click on Next when you have made your choice.
5. Sort your fields in the next window, then in subsequent windows

choose your layout and styles, then finally give your report a title.

6. Click on the <u>F</u>inish button when all the options have been chosen (you can go back using the <u>B</u>ack button to amend your choices). The report created is displayed (Figure 5.18). This report has

Title	Last Name	Publisher
Digital Photography	Bargh	Hodder and Stoughton
e-Learning Skills	Clarke	Palgrave Macmillan
Evaluating Training		
Programs	Kirkpatrick	Berrett-Koehler
General Lee	Taylor	University of Nebraska Press
Gettysburg	Bicheno	Cassell
Online Education	Kearsley	Wadsworth
The Futurians	Knight	John Day
With Pen and Saber	Trout	Stackpole

Figure 5.18 Report display

Activity   Report

Create a report that displays the Title, ISBN number and Date of Publication in this order. Sort your report by the Title in an ascending way. Give your report the title 'Basic information'.

Feedback
A sample report is shown in Figure 5.19. The report 'Basic information' would then be listed in the References window when the Report option was chosen.

Basic information

Title	ISBN number	Date of Publication
Digital Photography	0340867493	2003
e-Learning Skills	01403917558	2004
Evaluating Training Programs	01576750425	1998
General Lee	0803294255	1994
Gettysburg	0304356980	2001
Online Education	0534506895	2000
The Futurians	0381982882	1977
With Pen and Saber	0811719308	1995

Figure 5.19 ISBN report display

selected the Title, Last names of author and Publisher of the books to display. This can then be printed.

The overall process in earlier versions of Access is very similar except that the initial database window is presented with the options along the top so that the Reports tab needs to be selected and then the New button. This will reveal a window with the Report Wizard option.

▶ Relational databases

A major feature of a database is the ability to show the relationships between tables of information. In our examples, we have created individual tables of data which are not related to each other. Although this can be useful, building tables with relationships provides considerable potential in organizing information. Remember, our aim is to produce a reference database to store details of books, papers and websites that you have located during your studies.

To create a relational database we need to prepare in a different way. We need to consider how to construct tables that relate to each other. What are the common features of the information? One is the name of the author, which links books, papers and websites. Table 5.3 shows the new tables. The table Author links to a second

Table 5.3 Relational database

Table	Field Name	Data Type
Author	Author Number	Autonumber
Author	First Name	Text – 25 characters
Author	Last Name	Text – 25 characters
Author	Comments	Memo
Content	Number	Number
Content	Title	Text – 50 characters
Content	Journal Title	Text – 35 characters
Content	Publisher	Text – 35 characters
Content	Page	Number
Content	URL	Text – 60 characters
Content	ISBN number	Text – 25 characters
Content	Date of Publication	Number
Content	Place of publication	Text – 25 characters
Content	Comments	Memo

table Content which contains information on books, papers and website material that the authors have written. The link is created by giving each author a unique number using the autonumber data type in the Author table, then transferring this number to the Content table.

A new blank database called 'Relational References' is created, then the tables are produced in the same way as individual tables to make the database window. Once you have the tables, you need to create the relationship between them. With the Relational References database loaded:

1. Select the Tools menu and the Relationships option to reveal the Relationships window which allows you to link different fields between tables.
2. Highlight the field you wish to link, then drag the link to the related field in the other table. In this case the relationship is between Item Number (Author) and Author Number (Content). This is shown in Figure 5.20. The same process is required in earlier versions of Access (such as 97).

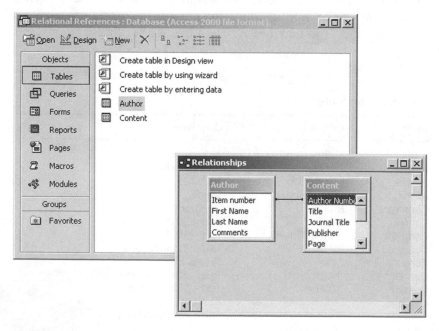

Figure 5.20 Access relationships

Information is entered into the tables in the normal way, then you can use reports, sorting and other functions. The query function can operate on both tables. If you wanted to display all the items written by a particular author, you could design a query to undertake this task.

Figure 5.21 shows the design of a query covering the two tables. The query creator has chosen to display Title, Publisher and Date of Publication from the Content table but only those items with an item number 1 in table Author. This is achieved by setting a criterion of 1 so that only the records relating to item 1 are displayed. The choice has also been made not to display the item number by removing the tick from the row Show. The query was saved and called 'Relation example'. Figure 5.22 displays the outcomes of this query.

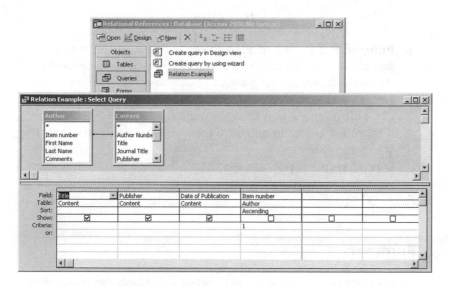

Figure 5.21 Designing a query

Title	Publisher	Date of Publication
e-Learning Skills	Palgrave Macmillan	2004
Online Learning and Social Exclusion	NIACE	2002
Designing Computer-Based Learning Materials	Gower	2001

Figure 5.22 Outcome of query access

► Alternative ways of creating tables

There is an alternative to creating a database when you simply want to produce a table of information. You can create an Excel spreadsheet in which you can sort the information in ascending and descending order, and locate specific information using the Find option in the Edit menu.

Excel can be effective if you need to create a single table of information quickly and do not want to produce specific reports or queries. However, bear in mind that once your list becomes substantial, it can be quite difficult to locate individual items of information or related items. Spreadsheets are effective as long as your table is short and does not need to relate to other information.

Top tips

1. **Planning:** it is vital to plan the structure and the data that you need your database to contain. A few days considering the options and thinking about what you want to achieve will be time well spent.
2. **Checking:** check that the information you enter is accurate. It takes far longer to amend a mistake than to ensure that it is initially correct.
3. **Queries and reports:** save them all. You will find that you will want to use them again.

► Summary

1.   Create a new blank database: select the Blank Database option in the New File display on the right-hand side of the display.
2.   Save a new blank database: save the new blank database in a folder of your choice using a meaningful name with the extension .mdb: this indicates an access database.
3.   Create a table: from the database window select Create Table in Design View to open the table window in which you can enter fields and data types, or select Create Table by using Wizard to open the Table Wizard.
4.   Edit table: highlight the table and select the Design option on the toolbar to open the table in Design View so you can add, remove and edit fields.

5. Enter data into a table: double-click on the table and it will open so you can type in your data.
6. Edit a field: click within the field so you can add, delete or change the information.
7. Delete a column: highlight the column and then select the Edit menu and the Delete Column option.
8. Highlight record: select the Edit menu and the Select Record option.
9. Highlight all the records: select the Edit menu and the Select All Records option.
10. Change table font: select the Format menu and the Font option.
11. Format table: select the Format menu and the Datasheet option to reveal the Datasheet Formatting window.
12. Change row height: select the Format menu and the Row Heights option to reveal the Row Height window.
13. Change column height: select the Format menu and the Column Widths option to reveal the Column Width window.
14. Change column name: select the Format menu and the Rename Column option.
15. Add new record: select the Insert menu and the New record option.
16. Add new column: select the Insert menu and the Column option.
17. Sort information: click in the column that you wish to sort and then select the Sort Ascending or Descending icon on the Table Datasheet toolbar.
18. Find information: select the Edit menu and the Find option to reveal the window entitled Find and Replace.
19. Move around table: select the Edit menu and highlight the Go To option to reveal a series of choices.
20. Filtering: highlight a specific field and then click on the Filter by Selection icon.
21. Printing: select the File menu and the Print option to reveal the Print window.
22. Query: select the Query option in the Database window and either Create Query in Design View or Create Query by using Wizard.
23. Reports: select the Reports option in the Database (References) window and choose from the options.
24. Relationships: select the Tools menu and the Relationships option to reveal the Relationships window that allows you to link different fields between tables.

6 Presenting (Microsoft PowerPoint®)

▶ Overview

It is a normal part of education to make presentations to explain your analysis of a topic. This can take a number of different forms, from a brief informal talk to your study group to the formal presentation of a project to your peers and tutors. This may be the first time that you have been asked to present information to an audience. Most people find presenting difficult and are anxious about how to carry out the task.

Microsoft PowerPoint® is a presentation application that will help you produce high-quality visual aids, speaking notes and handouts, thus enabling you to deliver a professional presentation. It helps you to prepare systematically for the event.

▶ Introduction

This chapter will concentrate on helping you to use Microsoft Power-Point® as an effective tool in making presentations as part of your course or research work. The chapter will cover:

- designing slides
- creating, copying, moving and deleting slides
- producing masters (that is, using standard layouts and colours)
- inserting objects (such as clipart and pictures) including using the drawing toolbar to create flowcharts
- adding charts to your slides
- adding effects such as slide transitions and animation
- producing handouts
- speaking notes
- presentation tips.

Microsoft PowerPoint® is used extensively in education, business and government to make presentations in various contexts. Sales staff present the benefits of their products to potential customers, teachers employ PowerPoint to enhance their classes, managers use it to help explain new developments to their employees and students present their work to their tutors.

Figure 6.1 shows the interface of Microsoft PowerPoint® 2002 with a presentation being developed. The current slide being edited is shown in the centre and right of the screen, while the other slides are displayed down the left-hand side when the Slides tab has been selected. At the bottom of the display, beneath the current slide, is a window showing the instruction 'Click to add notes'. This lets you write speaking notes relative to the slide you will be using as a visual aid. The interface is broadly similar to other Microsoft® Office applications, with toolbars and menu bar across the top of the window and status information across the bottom (for example, slide 2 of 7).

Earlier versions of PowerPoint (such as PowerPoint 97) simply present the current slide in the working area. The right and left-hand columns are not displayed and speaker notes are not visible. To add speaker notes in PowerPoint 97 you need to select the View menu

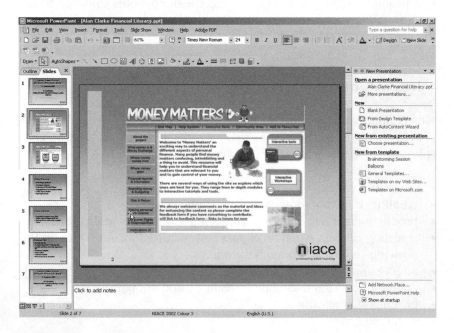

Figure 6.1 Microsoft PowerPoint®

and Speaker Notes option to reveal a window in which you can enter your notes. You can view the slide and its notes together by choosing the Notes Page option. The slides and outline of the presentation can be seen by selecting the View menu and Slide sorter or Outline, respectively.

On the left-hand side (again see Figure 6.1) alongside the Slides tab is a second tab called Outline. If you click this tab, next to a display of slides you will be shown the text that appears on each slide.

► How PowerPoint can help you overcome presentation anxiety

It is normal to feel anxious when you are required to do a presentation. The key to helping yourself overcome presentation anxiety is preparation. PowerPoint on its own will not turn you into a competent public speaker, but it will ensure that you develop:

- a reasonable structure for your talk
- a good set of visual aids
- handouts to give a professional appearance to your presentation
- speaking notes.

If you are new to public speaking, it is very easy to become so nervous that you become confused or forget to explain key points in your talk. If you prepare a presentation in advance you will have a structure to follow. Visual aids help audiences understand presentations, so by using PowerPoint you are assisting your listeners' understanding. If you develop handouts based on your presentation, you are again aiding your audience to follow your reasoning, no matter how you feel on the day of the presentation. Finally, a set of speaking notes that relate to each slide will allow you to overcome any reliance on your memory.

Microsoft PowerPoint® will not guarantee a successful presentation but it can eliminate some of the factors that can lead to a poor one.

► Design

Designing visual aids is a straightforward task, providing you are aware of some basic good practice. The key factors are:

- Slides should be simple displays of information. It is important to avoid overly complex slides. They are not intended to display all the information that you are presenting. They are most effective when they emphasize the key points of the message.
- Lists or bullet points are easier to read and recognize as distinct issues than is a paragraph of text, so are ideal for slides where you are seeking to stress the important items.
- When preparing PowerPoint slides, it is natural to want to use colour to make your presentation attractive and motivate listeners to pay attention. However, to ensure readability you need to maximize the contrast between the text and the background colour. When designing slides on a screen you can sometimes be misled about contrast because the colours will change when the slides are projected through a video projector or printed on overhead projector transparencies (made of acetate). There is no substitute for trying out the slides and observing how they appear. View your slides from the back of the room where your presentation will be held. This will help you check contrast, readability and appearance.
- Slides are intended to help you communicate your message to an audience. Pictures are often an effective means of conveying ideas, content and themes. They can emphasize, draw attention, motivate and communicate complex subjects in a single image. Nevertheless, they are best used in a simple, straightforward way.
- It may seem surprising but the readability of a slide is often improved by the amount of white or empty space that you leave on the slide. It is therefore good practice to leave the majority of the slide empty. Approaches such as leaving an empty line between bullet points can be very effective.
- Highlighting key information is an important part of any slide. You can do this by varying:
  - the character size between heading, bullet points and other text
  - fonts to draw attention to particular pieces of information.
- PowerPoint provides numerous different effects and animations to include in your presentations. They are useful aids to attracting attention to particular elements of the slides, but the key to effective practice is not to over-use them.
- Consistency throughout the presentation will help your audience understand your subject, since they will know where on the slide

you place your headings, images and other features. This helps them to identify quickly the information they are seeking.

Figure 6.2 is an example of a simple slide which follows the good practice guidelines above in that:

- it has a simple display of four key points
- points are listed to aid readability and understanding
- colour is used to gain interest but text and background colours maximize contrast (the slide uses black on yellow)
- the picture is used to emphasize the overall theme of presentations to draw the audience's attention
- the slide has a lot of white space to aid readability
- the main heading uses a larger character size and a different colour than other text to emphasize their differences
- the slide displays each bullet point separately so that individual points can be discussed and a list built up during the presentation.

Figure 6.2 Visual aid

▶ Worked example

To provide a focus throughout the chapter a worked example is provided which follows the discussion of PowerPoint functions. It is based on a student presentation, in which the students have been asked to present the outcomes of an assignment that they have undertaken.

This student has investigated the organization of AnyTown Community College, which provides adult education opportunities to people living within a three-mile radius of the site. The assignment forms a significant part of the student's assessment for the module.

▶ Creating, copying, moving and deleting slides

When you initially open Microsoft PowerPoint® 2002 it presents you with a blank slide that is designed to act as a title for the presentation. It has two boxes with the following messages:

- Click to add title.
- Click to add subtitle.

Other versions of PowerPoint have a different opening display. Power-Point 97 opens with a window in the centre of the display which allows you to select the option to:

- use Autocontent Wizard
- use a template
- create a new blank presentation
- open an existing presentation.

These options are also available within PowerPoint 2002, and can be accessed from the list of options on the right-hand side of the display (see Figure 6.1). This chapter will use PowerPoint 2002, but you will find that you can use the same methods in any version of the application, although the functions will sometimes be displayed in different screen locations.

Creating a slide
To create the title slide:

1. Open PowerPoint to reveal the initial display.

2. Click within either of the two boxes (Click to add title or Click to add subtitle) and enter text from the keyboard. In PowerPoint 97 you need to select the Blank presentation option to reveal the new slide window from which you can choose the title slide layout. For our worked example, the title is AnyTown Community College and my name is the subtitle. The text will appear in black and the background is white (or transparent if you print the slides on acetate overhead projector film).

3. Add a background colour by selecting the Format menu and the option Background from the drop-down menu. This will reveal the Background window, and the full range of colours can be shown by clicking on the drop-down arrow and then on the More Colors option.

4. Choose a colour from those shown in the new box. It can be selected by clicking on the OK button, then on the Apply or Apply to All buttons in the background window. Apply will select the colour for the current slide only, while Apply to All will select a background colour for all the slides. You can select or change a colour at any time during the creation of the presentation. The process is the same in earlier versions of PowerPoint.

5. Change the text colours by highlighting the text and selecting the Format menu then the Font option which will open the Font window. This lets you change the font, font style, character size, text effects (such as underlining) and colour of text. The same functions are available in earlier versions of PowerPoint.

6. Add a new slide once you have created your title slide by selecting the Insert menu and the New Slide option. This will open a new blank slide and a wide variety of layouts including:
   • text only
   • pictures only
   • text and pictures.
   The slide layout options are presented on the right of the display.

7. Select the layout you want by clicking on the option in the window to the right of the slide area (Figure 6.3).

After you have selected a slide, your presentation will consists of two slides, and you can move between them by clicking on the miniature representations of them on the left of the slide area or by using the scroll bar (Figure 6.1). An alternative way of viewing all the slides within the presentation is to select the View menu and the Slide Sorter option to reveal thumbnail images of the slides (Figure 6.3). Figure 6.3

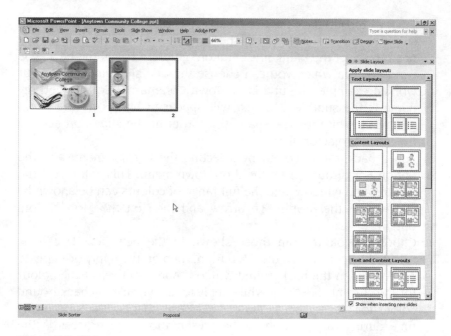

Figure 6.3 Slide sorter

shows the first two slides for the worked example presentation. The sequence of the slides within the presentation can be changed by dragging and dropping them, and additional slides can be inserted using the Insert menu and the New Slide option. Slides can also be deleted by highlighting them and pressing the delete key, or using the Edit menu and the Delete Slide option.

Design templates

Microsoft PowerPoint® includes a wide range of design templates from which to choose. These provide attractive presentation designs so that you do not need to consider colours or layout. They are accessed from the opening display by selecting either the options:

- From Design Template: this opens on the right-hand side of the display a series of illustrations of the templates available. You select one by clicking on your choice, which is then loaded into the current slide.
- General Templates: this opens a window with a list of the templates available, and you select by double-clicking. A single click will allow you the opportunity to view the template within the window.

Activity   Explore the options

Open Microsoft PowerPoint® and select a template for the worked example of a presentation of an assignment which has investigated the organization of Anytown Community College. Design the title slide.

Feedback
This presentation creator began by thinking about what he was going to tell the audience about the assignment. He wrote some notes about the overall objective and the purpose of the opening slide. It had three main purposes:

* to gain the attention of the audience
* to explain the assignment's objectives
* to introduce the speaker.

A few minutes spent considering what you are aiming to achieve will help you design effective visual aids.

This sample presentation has selected the proposal template, since it presents an attractive interface with background images of a clock and a pile of papers. This is appropriate in that the clock brings up associations of college timetables, and the papers of libraries or studying.

To create the slide, first click in the title boxes and enter 'Anytown Community College' for the title, and the presenter's name for the subtitle. A line under Anytown will indicate that the spelling checker does not recognize the word. You can ignore the line since it will not be projected or printed.

(This slide has also removed the black border around the words by selecting the Format menu and the Placeholder option to reveal the format autoshapes window. Select the Line Color drop-down button and the No Line option.)

Figure 6.4 shows the sample opening slide. What did you do?

Figure 6.4 Title slide

Activity   Explore the options – *continued*

Once the title slide has been designed, it is necessary to determine what to say to introduce the presentation. This is the kind of thing that would be appropriate:

> My name is Alan Clarke and this presentation is the outcome of an assignment to investigate the organization of AnyTown Community College. The college serves the adults who live within three miles of the site.

This text can be added to the slide notes window.

A third option which will achieve the same outcome as from Design Template is to select the Format menu and the Slide Design option. In earlier versions of PowerPoint (such as 97), Presentation Designs are available by selecting the Format menu and Apply Design option.

▶ Masters

It is good practice to employ a consistent style for your slides (with standard layouts, text and colours), and this can be achieved using slide masters in Microsoft PowerPoint®. In a presentation you need to develop two types of master, a title and a slide master. You can create a blank master or one based on a template. In both cases:

1. Select the slide format/template.
2. Select the View menu and highlight the Master option to reveal three additional options, Slide, Handout and Note Master. The process is the same in earlier versions of PowerPoint. Figure 6.5 shows the slide master that will appear if it is selected from the title slide produced in the previous activity.

Figure 6.5 shows you how to edit the default values of the slide master by clicking on the object you want to change. If you click in the title area at the top of the slide you will find that it uses Arial, size 36 font. Similarly in the object area, the bullet points use Arial, sizes 32, 28 (second level), 24 (third level), 20 (fourth level) and 20 (fifth level). The different bullet styles are shown. At the bottom of the display are three areas, date, footer and number.

Once you have made your changes, save the presentation.

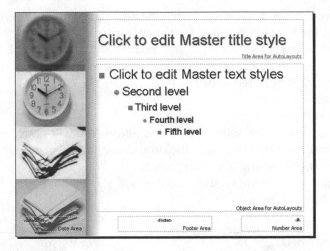

Figure 6.5 Slide master

Activity   Create a slide master

Starting from your title slide for the Anytown presentation, create a slide master. Edit the different areas to produce the effects that you are seeking. Save your presentation.

Feedback
Changing the font between the heading text and the main body of the slide is often a useful attention-directing device, since the audience will be drawn by the difference, and also realize the difference is associated with differing messages. You might for example change the font in the object area (main body) to Comic Sans MS, reduced the number of bullet levels to two, and alter the style of the bullets.

Create a second slide

In order to add a second slide to the Anytown presentation after creating the slide master, you need to:

1. Select the View menu and the Slide Sorter option.
2. Select the Insert menu and the New Slide option, and you will see a new slide added.
3. Choose a slide layout from those displayed on the right-hand side of the display. This is the same process in earlier versions of PowerPoint

except the layout is selected from the new slide window which opens when the New Slide option is chosen. Figure 6.3 shows the choices.

4. Select a layout by placing your pointer over it to reveal a down arrow button which, if clicked, will open to reveal three choices:
   - Apply to Selected Slides
   - Reapply Layout
   - Insert New Slide.

   In this case select Apply to Selected Slides. You will notice that you can insert a new slide from the drop-down layout menu. This is an alternative to using the Insert menu.

5. Open the new slide so that you can add text by double-clicking on the slide.

Activity   Create a second slide

Create a second slide for the Anytown presentation. The first step is to consider what you want to say to your audience after you have introduced yourself and your presentation. What layout will be most appropriate for your message? You also need to create your speaking notes – you may find it best to decide on them first. However, different speakers prefer different routes. Some like to create the visual aids and then the notes, while others prefer the opposite order.

Feedback
After the opening title slide I would suggest that you need to tell your audience what your presentation will cover. The title and text layout needs to be one appropriate for presenting a list of items related to the content of the presentation. A suitable heading is 'Content', and you could opt for six bullet points:

1. Assignment objectives.
2. College organization.
3. Strategic plan.
4. Staff views.
5. Adult learners' views.
6. Conclusions.

Here are some sample speaking notes to accompany this slide:

> During my presentation I shall explain my assignment objectives and the approach that I took to carry out the work. This included:
>
> 1. An analysis of the college's strategic plan.
> 2. Consideration of the college's organization to deliver the plan.
> 3. The views so that the staff about how well the college meets the needs of their community.
> 4. The views of the adult learners who attend the college courses.
> 5. The conclusions that I reached after undertaking the investigation.

▶ **Pictures**

In any presentation the use of pictures is vital since it will create interest, provide an alternative to text and allow you to summarize a lot of
content in a single image. PowerPoint enables you to insert clip art,
pictures you have created with a painting application or photographed
with a digital camera, and screen images you have captured. They are
inserted into your presentation in the same way.

If you select one of the many layouts containing a picture, you will see
on your slide the message 'Click icon to add content' with the picture icon.
The box contains six small icons that represent different forms of image:

- table
- chart
- clip art
- picture
- diagram or organizational chart
- media clip (sound or video).

To select the content, click on the icon of the image you want to insert, and
each will take you to the appropriate location to achieve your outcome. In
earlier versions of PowerPoint (such as 97), you need to select the Insert
menu and highlight the Picture option to reveal the options. Later we shall
consider charts and pictures, but for the moment let us consider clip art.

If you select the clip art icon, a window will open allowing you to
search for the appropriate image for your slide.

You can also insert images into slides that do not include pictures by
selecting the Insert menu and highlighting the Picture option to reveal
another menu. This shows several options related to inserting images.
These are:

- Clip Art.
- From File: this allows you to insert images stored in a folder.
- From Scanner or Camera: you can insert images taken with a
  camera or scanned into the computer.
- New Photo Album: this lets you create a collection of images for
  your presentation.
- Organization Chart: to create a chart within your presentation.
- Autoshapes: allows you to insert many standard images (such as
  arrows).
- WordArt: enables you to create text which is curved, bent or rotated
  in various ways.

Another way of inserting or creating slide images is by using the drawing toolbar. You can create lines of different thickness, change the colour of areas, text and lines, insert three-dimensional shapes, add shadows, and be creative.

Activity   Create the third slide

Create a third slide for the Anytown presentation. In your second slide you have explained the content of the presentation and revealed that you will explain your objective for the assignment, so your third slide needs to focus on the objective. It would be appropriate to include either a picture of the college itself (which you might take with a digital camera) or a piece of clip art, the option we shall pursue.

Feedback
Using the slide layouts, you might choose one with a picture on the right-hand side and text on the left. If your search for 'college' does not locate any useful images, you might try the word 'building' or other alternatives. An image can be dragged to change its size, position or orientation using the mouse pointer and the framework surrounding the image. If you cannot see a framework, a single click on the artwork will reveal it.
    The sample slide heading is Objective, and the text is:

    To investigate the operation of the Community College to determine if it meets the needs of the local community.

There is a picture on the right of a college building.
    The sample speaking notes are:

    My objective was to consider if the programmes provided by the college were suitable for the local community, in particular adults living within a three-mile radius of the college. This objective was agreed with my tutor.

▶ Charts

There are several ways of inserting an organizational chart into a slide, such as: selecting the Insert menu and highlighting the Picture option to reveal another menu of options that includes an organizational chart. Alternatively, you can insert a new slide (using the New Slide option in the Insert menu) and then choose the Organization Chart layout. This inserts a blank slide with an icon in the middle and with the instruction to double-click to add a diagram or organization chart. When you double-click, you open the Diagram Gallery window. This allows you to choose from a range of diagrams by clicking on them. Clicking places an outline chart in the slide, with a toolbox (Figure 6.6). The toolbox lets you add extra cells, add lines and manipulate the chart.

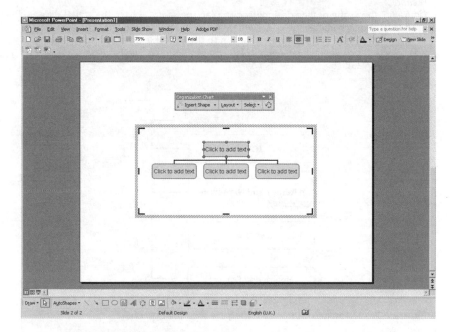

Figure 6.6 Organization Chart and Toolbox

Activity

Create a fourth slide for the Anytown presentation. In your second slide you have explained the content of the presentation and revealed that you considered the organizational structure of the college. In this slide you will create an organizational chart of the college. The chart should show that:

1. The college is managed by a principal.
2. There are four departments organized by subject area: ICT, Literacy and Numeracy, Leisure, and Health and Fitness.

To change the size or font, highlight the text and select the font and size. The chart cells will adjust to fit the new text. Remember your slides need to be read from the back of the room which may be some distance from the front, so select a large character size.

Activity   *continued*

Feedback
Figure 6.7 shows the outline design used to plan the sample chart. The actual slide used Arial and a character size of 32, which should be visible many feet from the front of the room. In order to fit the chart on to the available area, a hanging display was selected. It could have been either left or right hanging. The heading is 'Organization: College'.

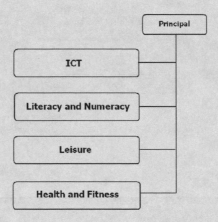

Figure 6.7 Anytown Community College – organization chart

The sample speaking notes are:

The college is managed by a principal and is divided into four departments. These are:

1. Information and Communication Technology, which provides introductory and intermediate programmes aimed at local people who use ICT for social and business activities.
2. Literacy and Numeracy, offering help to adults with poor reading, writing and number skills.
3. Leisure, which offers a wide range of courses for people who want to learn for its own sake. The courses cover foreign languages, local history, genealogy, philosophy and many other areas. Many of the courses take place in community locations in local villages.
4. Health and Fitness, providing keep fit programmes at many different levels (for example for the over 70s) and a wide variety of sporting activities.

Once you have created a few slides, you will need to check how they will appear as a presentation. In order to run the presentation from the beginning, select the Slide Show menu and the View Show option.

To display the presentation from the slide shown, click on the Slide Show button in the bottom left-hand corner of the display. Whichever option you choose, the slides fill the screen, and you can move through them by clicking the mouse button or by pressing the enter key. When you pass the final slide, the screen will blank and you will see the instruction 'End of Slide Show: Click to Exit'. Click the mouse button to return to PowerPoint. In earlier versions of PowerPoint the process is very similar.

▶ Transitions and animation

During a presentation, you may want to add interest or build up your story by revealing each part of your slide as you explain that element of your presentation. This helps you keep your audience focused on what you are saying. Microsoft PowerPoint® provides a range of devices to animate your slides or use special effects. The best advice for using animation and effects is to employ them sparingly. If you use too many effects, you will simply distract your audience from your presentation.

Animations is the term used for the way the content of the slides appears. The text can, for example, appear slowly one line at a time (fade in one by one) or move up or down the screen (ascend or descend). Transitions refer to the way that one slide changes into the next. To access both animations and transitions:

1. Highlight the slide or the object (such as text) on the slide.
2. Select the Slide Show menu to reveal the options: Animation Schemes and Slide Transition. You can have a consistent pattern of effects throughout your presentation, or different ones for each slide.
3. Select either Animation Schemes (called Preset Animation in Power-Point 97) or Slide Transition, to reveal a list of options in a scrolling window on the right of the display (such as Fade in All, Fade in One by One, Blinds Vertical and Cover Left).
4. Select the effect of your choice by clicking on it. You will notice that there are buttons that allow you to:

- apply to all slides the animation or transition you have chosen
- view the slide show
- add timings to the transition from one slide to another
- play the current slide animation or transition.

Activity   Transitions and animation

Using the presentation you have been creating, experiment with the different transition and animation effects. You will need to run the presentation to observe many of the effects, or use the Play button. However, when you select an option you will see it applied to your current slide, and you can judge its effects if the AutoPreview button is ticked.

Feedback
It would be sensible to decide that the transition between slides should be standardized throughout the presentation, so that the audience will not be distracted by too many changes. You might choose the Newsflash option for this presentation, since it will gain the attention of the audience and clearly distinguish between slides, although you could equally well decide on another option.

Animation would only be suitable for some slides, so the sample presentation takes these choices:

1. In the title slide there is no animation since there is no need to animate the title. Animation combined with the Newsflash option would have been too much.
2. Slide Two, Content: it would be effective to have each item appear separately, so you can speak about them individually and thus systematically build up the discussion. Select the Appear option after highlighting the text box. Each bullet will appear after you have clicked the mouse button.
3. Slide Three, Objective: again, it would be effective for the slide initially to appear showing just the heading 'Objective' and the picture. The actual text appears after the mouse button is clicked.
4. Slide Four, Organization Chart: there is not really a reason for the slide to be animated. The chart itself should draw sufficient attention from the audience.

▶ **Final slides**

In order to complete the presentation, we need to create four more slides to cover the strategic plan, adult learners' views, staff views and conclusions. Figure 6.8 shows the remaining four slides.

Speaking notes

These are suggested speaking notes for each of the four final slides.

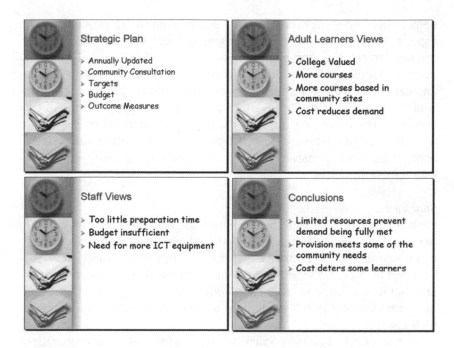

Figure 6.8 Final slides

Strategic Plan
The college produces an annual Strategic Plan after a process of consulting the local people. This is undertaken by organizing an open weekend at the college when people are given the opportunity to learn about the courses that are planned for the next year. They can take part in taster sessions to see if a course would appeal to them.

The Strategic Plan contains targets for the college to meet in terms of the number of learners who will participate in programmes and the proportion of them that will complete the courses. The budget for the college is included so that the community can make a judgement of the value for money it is receiving. The final section covers outcome measures by which the college can judge its success (such as learner satisfaction, which is measured through an end of course evaluation form).

Adult Learners' Views
The learners that I interviewed clearly valued the college. They all had stories about how it had helped them or their friends and

neighbours. They wanted the college to expand its provision and especially to provide more programmes in local sites so that they did not need to travel to the main college location. The problem was that many residents relied on public transport, and this was very limited and expensive even for short journeys. The added factor was that in winter many people did not want to be too far away from home in the evenings. The other limiting factor was cost. Courses were free if you were in receipt of means-tested benefits but for others they were sometimes too expensive. This led to some people being unable to take part.

Staff Views

I was able to meet several members of staff, and they were very proud of working in the Community College, believing that their work helped many people enrich their lives. However, they felt strongly that the college's budget was insufficient to meet the needs of the local people, and that this resulted in teachers having too little preparation time and inadequate access to ICT equipment to help them prepare or to use in their courses.

The college relied on the good will of the staff to undertake preparation and other tasks in their own time.

Conclusions

I reached the following conclusions in respect of my objective, which to remind you was:

> To investigate the operation of the Community College to determine if it meets the needs of the local community.

My conclusions are:

1. Limited resources prevent demand being fully met.
2. Provision meets some of the community needs.
3. Cost deters some learners.

▶ Spellchecker

A common fear when presenting using visual aids is that you have made spelling mistakes. PowerPoint provides the means of checking the spelling of your slides. To do this:

1. Select the Tools menu.
2. Select the Spelling option. This will open the Spelling window which operates in the same way as the spellchecker within Word. The process is the same in earlier versions of PowerPoint.

▶ Handouts

The purpose of any presentation is to convey information and understanding to your audience. An important element is the provision of a record of the presentation contents. PowerPoint enables you to turn your slides into different forms of handouts. In order to produce these:

1. Select the File menu and the Print option to reveal the Print window. The window offers you several choices such as:
   - Print what: slides, handouts, notes, pages and outline view.
   - Slides per page: from one to nine slides on each page. Three slides per page leaves a space for your audience to write notes.
   - Order: you can lay out the handout either horizontally or vertically.
2. Click on the Preview button before printing to check your choices.
3. Choose your print option and click on the OK button to print it. The options are:
   - The Slide option produces a copy of each slide, that is, one slide per page.
   - The Handout option offers you a range of choices. Figure 6.9 shows you three examples of handouts: one, six and three slides per page.
   - The Note Page option allows you to print copies of the slides including your speaking notes.
   - The Outline View option enables you to produce a copy of the text of all your slides.
   These options are available in earlier versions but the layout of the Print window is different.

Each of the options serves a different purpose in a presentation:

- Slides: allows you to give your audience full-size copies of the slides (one slide per page).
- Handouts: you can save paper while giving your listeners a copy of the slides. The three slides page with a space for notes is a useful alternative.

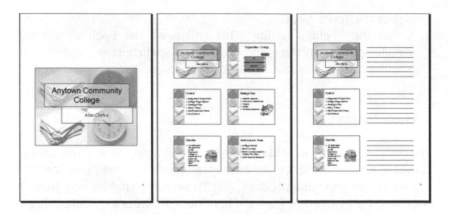

Figure 6.9 Handouts

- Note Page: lets you give copies of the slides and your speaking notes to your audience. This can also serve as your own notes.
- Outline View: this is probably more useful to you as a planning document, giving the opportunity to study the whole presentation.

All forms of the printouts can be produced in colour or black and white. If you have access to a colour printer, printing in colour will add considerable interest to your presentation.

▶ Presenting

Slides are an important part in your presentation, but on their own they will not produce a quality event. You need to use them in the most appropriate way. Here are some tips for a good presentation:

- Check the room by running the presentation while moving around to ensure that your slides can be seen by everyone. This will also show you where you ought to stand. It is very easy to block the view of your audience by standing or sitting in the wrong place.
- Check your slides by projecting them, since it is easy to be deceived by the appearance of your slides on the screen. You should always view them when they are projected. Colours will change, what appears to be an adequate character size will not be visible in a large room, and contrast may be inadequate.

- Position the computer monitor so that you can see the slides. This will act as a prompt to you without the need to turn your head to look at the main display. It is good practice to face your audience and not look at the main display too frequently.
- Make sure you know how to control the presentation (for example, start the presentation, move slides forward and back, and operate the video projector). It is wise to spend time trying out the equipment before the presentation.
- Use the slides to summarize what you are saying. It is poor practice to read them unless you are seeking to emphasize a particular point or to read out a quote.
- Leave your slides on display long enough to be read and understood. New speakers often change them too quickly in their anxiety, so try to give your audience plenty of time.
- Limit the number of slides. A common problem is to have too many slides for the time allocated for the presentation. (A rule of thumb is no more than two slides per minute.)
- Position yourself so that you can see a clock, place your watch where you can see it, or ask someone to time you. It is very difficult to know how long you have spoken without timing yourself.
- Give copies of the handouts to the audience before you start, or at least tell them that copies of the slides will be distributed at the end, so people don't waste time taking notes of the content. The advantage of giving people a copy of the sides before you start is that it allows them to annotate them with their own notes.

Top tips

1. **Audience:** probably the single most important item to consider when preparing for a presentation is the audience. Who are they? What do they want from the presentation?
2. **Simplicity:** Microsoft PowerPoint ® includes many features to provide a colourful and exciting presentation. However, good practice is to not over-use them. One animation will gain the audiences attention while ten will simply bore them.
3. **Handouts:** provide handouts so that the audience can add their own notes.
4. **Copies:** keep copies of your presentations then you can use them again. It is far easier to modify a successful presentation than to create a new one.

▶ **Summary**

1. Background colour: select the Format menu and the option Background from the drop-down menu. This will reveal the Background window, and the full range of colours can be shown by clicking on the drop-down arrow and then on the More Colors option.

2. Text colours: highlight the text and select the Format menu and the Font option which will open the Font window and allow you to change the font, font style, character size, text effects and colour of text.

3. View all slides: select the View menu and the Slide Sorter option to reveal thumbnail images of the slides.

4. Change the sequence of the slides: within slide sorter, drag and drop slides to change the order of display.

5. Add new slides: select the Insert menu and the New Slide option.

6. Delete slides: highlight the slide then select the Edit menu and the Delete Slide option.

7. Design templates: select from the illustrations on the right-hand side of the display or select the Format menu and the Slide Design option.

8. General templates: select from the list of the templates displayed in the window by double-clicking.

9. Slide master: select the View menu and highlight the Master option to reveal three additional options: Slide, Handout and Note Master.

10. Pictures: select a layout containing a picture, then you will see on your slide the message 'Click icon to add content' with the picture icon.

11. Pictures: select the Insert menu and highlight the Pictures option to reveal another menu.

12. Drawing toolbar: allows you to insert images, autoshapes, shapes (such as a rectangle), create lines of different thickness, change the colour of areas, text and lines, insert three-dimensional shapes, add shadows and be creative.

13. Organization chart: select the Insert menu and highlight the Picture option to reveal another menu of options that allows you to insert an organizational chart. Alternatively select the Insert menu and the New Slide and choose the Organization Chart layout.

14.   Run the presentation: select the Sli<u>d</u>e Show menu and the <u>V</u>iew Show option or click on the Slide Show button in the bottom left-hand corner of the display.

15.   Animations and transitions: select the Sli<u>d</u>e Show menu to reveal the options – Animation S<u>c</u>hemes and Slide <u>T</u>ransition.

16.   Handouts: select the <u>F</u>ile menu and the <u>P</u>rint option to reveal the Print window.

7 Managing your system

▶ Overview

Information and communication technology can be a powerful aid to your studies and make a substantial contribution to your success. That said, to gain the most from your system, you must be able to control it. Computer problems can often distract you from gaining the benefits from the system, so it is therefore important that you understand how to use the system to reduce problems and maximize the advantages.

▶ Operating systems

Microsoft Windows® is the most widely used operating system in the world, and is available in a variety of versions:

- Windows 95
- Windows 98
- Windows ME
- Windows 2000
- Windows XP Home or Windows XP Professional.

You may be using any of these versions since they represent the development of the operating system over the past ten years. Windows 95 was launched in 1995, with Windows XP, the latest addition to the family, being launched in 2001. Between launches of completely new versions, Microsoft has provided upgrades in the form of service packs to add extra features and to resolve problems. These are normally available from the Microsoft website.

All the versions provide the same core functions that are discussed within this book. However, the presentation will vary and the later versions will offer more functionality. If you have bought a new computer recently, it is highly likely that if an operating system has been included, it is Windows XP. To identify your operating system, observe the screen displays as the computer starts up: the version is shown.

You can buy upgrade software to enhance your copy of Windows to one of the more advanced versions. This is cheaper than buying a full copy of the latest version.

Some colleges are also using an alternative operating system called Linux. This is a free system which was originally produced by Linus Torvalds. It is called an open source application: this means the source code is freely available for developers to modify or customize to their needs.

All versions of the Windows® operating system offer a range of functions that are fundamental to using a computer effectively. They include:

- a help system
- finding files and folders
- adjusting/adapting the system to meet your needs, especially if you are disabled
- managing your files and folders.

File management includes:

- creating, deleting and moving files and folders
- renaming files and folders
- recovering files that have been deleted by mistake
- organizing files and folders
- compressing and decompressing files.

This chapter will also cover some important aspects of managing your computer. These are:

- backing up your information
- protecting your information
- networks.

► Applications

Many applications are continuously evolving, with new versions being produced at regular intervals. The norm is that the latest versions will have more functions than earlier ones, and that the latest version will be compatible with all the earlier versions. However, documents, spreadsheets, images and other outputs of the newest edition may not be read by older versions.

Microsoft® Office has evolved through many different versions such as:

- Microsoft Office 97
- Microsoft Office 2000
- Microsoft Office XP (2002).

Microsoft® Office is the most widely used integrated package of word processing, spreadsheets and other applications. Microsoft provides different combinations of applications within Office such as Microsoft Office Standard and Microsoft Office Professional (which includes the Access database program). These are intended to appeal to different types of user. New versions of Microsoft® Office and other applications are also often available in upgrade form, so if you already own a version you can gain the improved functionality at a lower cost. The upgrade searches for an earlier edition of the product and then upgrades it. If it does not locate an earlier one it will not install.

Although Microsoft® Office is the dominant product in office applications, there are some alternatives which offer similar functionality, including:

- IBM Lotus SmartSuite (http://www.lotus.com/)
- Sun StarOffice (http://www.staroffice.com/)
- Ability Office (http://www.ability.com/)
- Microsoft Works (http://www.microsoft.com)
- OpenOffice (http://www.openoffice.org).

Many software providers offer student and teacher discounts to buyers of their products, allowing you to purchase the latest applications at a discount price. Suppliers will normally want you to prove your status, and if you are buying online they will usually look for an educational e-mail address (such as your college e-mail account).

► Help

All versions of Windows® provide users with a help system to assist with use of the operating system. It is available by clicking on the Start button to reveal a window of options, among which is Help.

The Windows Help system is concerned not only with assisting you to solve problems once you have encountered them, but also with aiding your understanding of the system by offering tutorials. Windows XP offers a range of tutorials covering subjects such as accessibility, printing and working remotely. In comparison, Windows 98 offers tutorials including Exploring Your Computer and Using Windows Accessories.

Windows provides you with a range of ways of using Help. These are:

- Contents: a list of subjects and topics from which you can select the one relevant to your needs
- Index: list of the topics covered by the system from which you can select
- Search: you enter keywords and they are matched to appropriate help topics.

Each version of Windows presents Help in a different way, so you may have to explore to develop your understanding of how your particular version operates. Figure 7.1 illustrates Help for Windows XP.

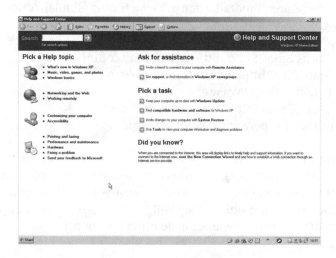

Figure 7.1 Windows XP Help

The information provided by the Help system can be printed, and it will often provide a system set of instructions to assist you carrying out a task.

Activity   Using Help

Click on the Start button and then on the Help option (called Help and Support in Windows XP and Help in Windows 98) to open the Help window.

1. Select one of the contents topics, click on the topic to access it, and consider how much assistance it provides to you.
2. Click on Index then scroll up and down the list to consider what is provided. Select an entry to find out more about the item.
3. Finally, use the search facility by entering some keywords. Attempt to find out how you can use a picture as the desktop background, or select another issue you are interested in.

Feedback
1. For a topic, you could pick music, video, games and photos. This leads you to a display where you can select the individual elements. If you choose music, this in turn is divided into a range of topics. If you pick playing and copying music, this leads to a list of possible tasks, tutorials and information about the subject.
2. The index is comprehensive, and should certainly make you feel that there is a great deal of information available. If you double-click on Mobility impairment, for example, you are presented with two sub-categories: Configuring Windows for people who have a mobility impairment, and Microsoft documentation in alternative formats. Selecting the first topic by double-clicking opens an introduction to the different ways Windows can be customized for people with mobility impairment.
3. For example, if you enter the keyword 'desktop' in Windows XP you will be presented with a list of 30 results. The list includes assistance with six tasks you might want to undertake (such as Use a picture as a desktop background), overviews (such as Creating shortcuts to files and folders), tutorials (such as Personalizing your workspace) and information (such as Introducing power management).

There is also a vast range of assistance available to you on the World Wide Web. The Microsoft website address is www.microsoft.com, and it contains a wealth of information and help. It has a section for college students at the moment at http://www.microsoft.com/Education/CollegeStudents.aspx. However, due to the dynamic nature of the World Wide Web this may have changed by the time you visit it.

▶ Customizing your system

Microsoft Windows® provides a variety of ways to customize the way information is presented to you, and how you interact with it.

Approximately 10 per cent of the population is left-handed, so one clear need is to be able to change the use of the mouse to make it suitable for left-handed use.

Mouse properties

Microsoft Windows® has functions to enable you to change the properties of the mouse. To access them:

1. Select the Control Panel and the Mouse option. This will open the Mouse Properties window.
2. Click on the radio button 'Switch primary and secondary buttons' to make the mouse suitable for left-handed users.
3. Confirm the choice by clicking on the OK button. The mouse properties window has a series of tabs to allow you to:
   - change the double-clicking speed
   - change the appearance of pointers (such as arrows and the hourglass)
   - change the speed of the pointer
   - change the effects of the mouse wheel operation (such as scrolling speed in relation to turning the wheel).

Display options

Microsoft Windows® has functions to assist you to change the display properties. To access the functions:

1. Select the Control Panel.
2. Choose the Display option to open the Display Properties window. The window has various tabs allow you to set:
   - themes: these are a group of related colours, icons and other effects which provide you with the means of individualizing the system
   - desktop: this allows you choose the background of the desktop
   - screen saver: this lets you choose between different screen savers
   - appearance: this enables you to change the appearance of aspects of the interface such as style, colour scheme and font size
   - settings: this allows you to change the resolution of the screen.

Accessibility options

Figure 7.2 shows the window in which you can enact the accessibility options. To access the functions:

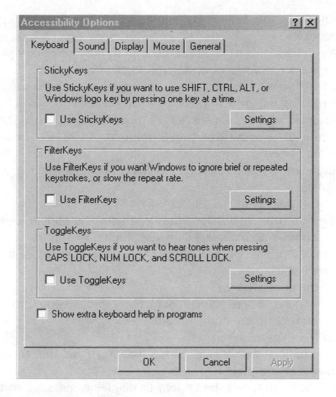

Figure 7.2 Accessibility options

1. Select the Control Panel.
2. Choose the Accessibility option. This will open the window in Figure 7.2. The various tabs are:
   - keyboard
   - sound
   - display
   - mouse
   - general.

   Each tab provides access to the functions which customize the system. The options are available in most versions of Windows.
3. Select the Keyboard tab in order to set:
   - StickyKeys: this is intended to help you press and hold down a key. If you need to use the Alt, Ctrl and Shift keys (all held down together) to end a process, with StickyKeys you only need to press each key once.

- FilterKeys: this helps you avoid accidentally pressing a key more than once.
- Togglekeys: this lets you set a sound to play when you press the Caps Lock, Num Lock and Scroll Lock keys.
4. Select the Sound tab to set two different functions for people who have hearing impairments. The two settings are:
   - SoundSentry: this causes part of the screen to blink in the application or window when an error occurs, instead of a sound being played.
   - ShowSounds: a text caption or icon appears when a sound is played.
5. Select the Display tab to set:
   - High Contrast: which provides you with the means to improve the contrast to aid users with visual impairment.
   - Cursor Options: where you can change the appearance and blink rate of the cursor.
6. Select the Mouse tab to set:
   - MouseKeys: where you can control the mouse pointer using the arrow keys on the number pad.
7. Select the General tab to set:
   - Automatic Reset: which allows you turn off the accessibility option after a period.
   - Notification: to set the system to display a message or make a sound when the accessibility feature is turned on or off.
   - SerialKey Devices: to use alternative input devices designed for disabled users.
   - Administrative Options: to apply accessibility options when you log on or set them as defaults.

▶ Accessories

Within the Accessories option in Windows XP (select the All Programs option in the Start menu) are several accessibility functions. Some earlier versions of the Windows operating system (such as Windows 97 and Windows 98) do not offer these functions. The accessibility functions include:

1. The Accessibility Wizard with which you can customize the settings of the system to meet your needs and preferences by selecting from lists of options.

Activity   Accessibility

Using the Control Panel accessibility options, explore the effects of making the changes.

Feedback
You can make many varied and significant changes. Probably the most dramatic change is the selection of High Contrast, which dramatically alters the display. There are many other things worth exploring such as:

1. Change the blink rate of the cursor from slow to fast to locate the pace you prefer. It can make a big difference to finding the cursor on the screen.
2. Try using the arrow keys on the number pad to control the on-screen pointer. Compare the process with using a mouse.
3. Explore the range of option settings in High Contrast: which did you prefer?

What did you discover?

2. The Magnifier, which provides an on-screen magnifying area to help you read the text displayed.
3. The Narrator, which is a text-to-speech system with fairly basic functionality. To investigate what it can do, select the option from the Accessibility menu and listen to Narrator read out the explanation that appears. You need to have a sound card, speakers or headphones to hear the speech.
4. The On-Screen Keyboard, which displays a keyboard you can employ to enter and edit text. Try to use it to form a judgement of how useful it could be to you.
5. The Utility Manager, which enables you to control the use of the other functions provided within Accessibility.

▶ Managing your files and folders

Modern computers are able to store enormous numbers of files, and can usefully hold complex folder structures, enabling you to have libraries of information available on your personal computer. However, this advantage does assume that you can locate the files when you want them. With hundreds of folders with thousands of files stored within them, it is not always easy to find what you need. The name you gave a file six months ago is unlikely to be remembered except in very general terms.

The best practice to help you locate a particular file is to name files and folders in a meaningful way.

Example
Don't call a file containing your second history assignment ABC123.txt, but rather historyassignment2.txt: the name will have some meaning to you.

Try to pick names with relevance so that you can identify them months later. The same approach is also required when naming folders, and it needs to be combined with an organized approach to their use. Use folders to separate out different topics, and do not randomly scatter them around your storage.

However, even these methods can fail. If they do, Windows provides a means of searching your system for particular files and folders. This is very useful. It is available within the Start button pop-up window in the option Search, which links you to the search results window. Earlier versions of Windows provided a similar func-tion called Find Files or Folders which was also available in the Start menu, although it was mainly limited to enabling you to locate files by their name.

The search results window enables you to search for a wide range of resources such as:

- pictures and sounds
- all types of files (such as word processing, spreadsheets, databases and PowerPoint)
- folders.

Organizing files and folders
The key to organizing your files and folders is to have a planned system, so you can locate the information you need when you need it. Windows lets you create new folders whenever you want, but this can lead you to a haphazard structure if you simply keep adding folders. A few minutes planning your structure will pay dividends later when you are struggling to locate files.

Figure 7.3 shows a folder structure for storing files relating to studying military history. There are a master folder called History, and four sub-folders within it called Boer War, WW1, WW2 and Korean War.

Activity   Searching

Try using the Search facility to locate a particular file or folder. Explore the different options that are available, such as searching for:

- files that were modified within last week, month, year, or simply you do not know
- the whole file name or just part of it
- a word or phrase contained in the file
- the file in a particular drive
- a file of a particular size
- files of a particular type (such as pictures).

Feedback
For example, you might need to search for a file called 'study skills' and not remember the last time it was modified. The search might locate four possible matches:

> ICT Skills for Studying C:\Documents 4,133 Kb Microsoft Word Doc 31/10/2004 14.25
> ICT Skills for Successful Study C:\Documents 3,926 Kb Microsoft Word Doc 24/10/2004 16.45
> ICT Skills for Studying C:\Documents 4,133 Kb Microsoft Word Doc 31/10/2004 14.25
> ICT Skills for Successful Study C:\Documents 3,926 Kb Microsoft Word Doc 24/10/2004 16.45

This search has actually found the same files twice over, so there are in effect two matches. The results provide details of where the files are located (the folder name), the size of the file, type of file (in this case, Microsoft Word documents) and the date and time they were last updated. Any of this information could be useful to help you decide which file is one you are looking for.
    What did you discover?

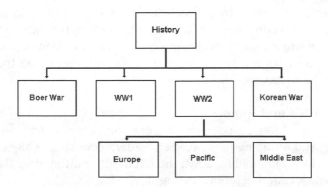

Figure 7.3 Folder structure

It could make sense to organize your work by the major themes of the course. Obviously you can continue to break down your files within the sub-folders into other folders. However, if you make your structure too deep, it can be difficult to remember where you saved your files, and prove almost as bad as having a single folder with everything dumped in it. There is no fixed rule about the depth of folder structure, but three levels will serve most purposes.

Example
Level 1 Master folder: History: overall subject
Level 2 Sub-folder: WW2: major theme of the subject
Level 3 Sub-sub-folder: Europe: significant part of WW2

Creating files and folders
It is possible to create files and folders within Windows using Windows Explorer, which is available in many versions of Microsoft Windows®. To open Windows Explorer in Windows XP:

1. Highlight the All Programs option in the Start window to open the menu.
2. Highlight the Accessories option to open a sub-menu.
3. Select the Windows Explorer option. (In earlier versions of Windows it is available in the Programs menu.) Figure 7.4 shows Windows Explorer in Windows XP. On the left side of the window you can see a list of folders.
4. Highlight a folder, and the files it contains are then shown on the right. In Figure 7.4 the folder My Documents is highlighted on the left, and on the right is a long list of folders and files stored within it.
5. Create a new folder by highlighting the folder or drive in which to place it, selecting the File menu, highlighting the New option to reveal a sub-menu, then clicking on the folder option. A new folder will appear within the Explorer window. You can name the folder from the keyboard.

Moving files and folders
Within the Explorer window you can drag and drop folders, as well as dragging and dropping files between folders. You simply highlight the chosen folder and, holding down the left mouse button, drag the folder to the new location before releasing it.

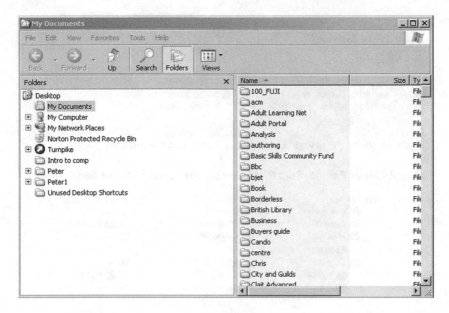

Figure 7.4 Windows Explorer

Activity   Creating folders

Using Windows Explorer, create the military folder structure discussed earlier.

Feedback
You could create the Military folder in the My Documents folder, and then add the sub-folders within the Military folder. Figure 7.5 illustrates the structure.

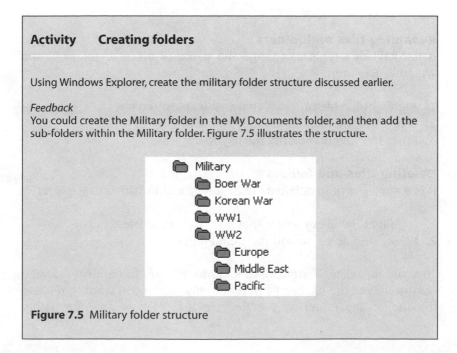

Figure 7.5 Military folder structure

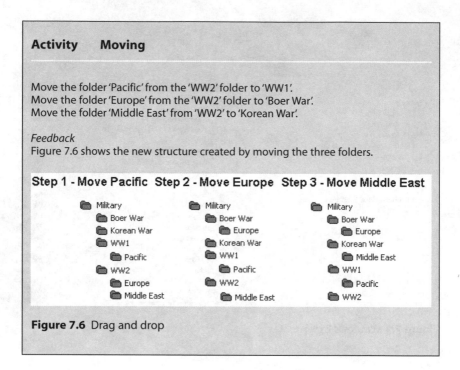

Activity   Moving

Move the folder 'Pacific' from the 'WW2' folder to 'WW1'.
Move the folder 'Europe' from the 'WW2' folder to 'Boer War'.
Move the folder 'Middle East' from 'WW2' to 'Korean War'.

Feedback
Figure 7.6 shows the new structure created by moving the three folders.

Figure 7.6 Drag and drop

Renaming files and folders

It is relatively simple to change the name of a file or folder within Windows Explorer:

1. Highlight the file or folder that you want to rename.
2. Select the File menu and the Rename option.
3. Enter the new name from the keyboard.

Deleting files and folders

It is a simple task to delete a file or folder within Windows Explorer:

1. Highlight the file or folder that you want to delete.
2. Select the File menu and the Delete option.

To avoid mistakes, a window appears to ask you to confirm that you want to delete the file or folder. It actually asks if you want to remove the file or the folder to the Recycle Bin. This is an area within

Windows to which deleted content is moved. If you later want to recover items from the Recycle Bin, you can. You therefore have a means of recovering files and folders that have been deleted by mistake.

Alternative methods

Microsoft Windows® offers various alternative means of undertaking tasks, and there are several ways of carrying out the renaming of a file. One is described above, using the menu options. Another is to right-click on the file name to open a menu with the option Rename. You can also left-click once on the file or folder, and after a short pause left click again. This will allow you to enter a new name.

The right-click menu also provides options to delete a file or folder, copy and paste it, and a number of other operations. Remember, many applications offer keyboard shortcuts so that you can directly access a menu function by pressing a combination of keys. They are shown by underlining (for example, New indicates that if you press Ctrl and N together you can carry out the function).

▶ Compressing and decompressing files

A key advantage of e-mail attachments is that you can send documents quickly. However, if an attachment is very large it can cause recipients problems. It can take a long time to download, especially if the addressee is based at home on a dial-up connection. Some networks place limits on the size of attachments they will receive, so it is important to control the size.

If you want to transport files on floppy disks or other media, you may also want to limit their size. Even using memory sticks with a large capacity there will be occasions when you need to reduce the size of files. In order to do this you can compress them using applications such as WinZip. This application also allows you to decompress a file so that you can read it. Compressing files is often called *zipping*, and decompressing is known as *unzipping*.

WinZip lets you create a compressed archive containing a number of files so that you can send them as a collection. An evaluation version of WinZip can be downloaded from the WinZip website (http://www. winzip.com/).

▶ Backing up your information

It is good practice while working on a computer to save your work regularly. This allows for the possibility that the computer will hang and you will lose your work. If you have saved it frequently, you will only lose a few minutes' effort. For similar reasons when you have a lot of files they should be saved on to a new medium, so that if your hard disk fails or your computer becomes infected by a virus, you have another copy of your files. This is like keeping a copy of an important letter. When studying, you do not want to lose what would take a great deal of effort to recreate. Another copy is always valuable.

This process of copying your files to another medium is called backing up. There are many ways of carrying out the operation. You can:

- create a CD-R/CD-RW containing your files
- create a DVD R/DVD-RW containing your files
- save your files to an external hard drive
- save your file on to a tape.

A simple approach is to create a CD-Rom using a write once or many times disc. This takes only a few minutes, and the product can be played on any computer with a CD-Rom drive, so your files can rapidly be accessed in the event of a disaster.

If your computer is part of a network, you can save your files to the network server as well as your machine's individual hard disc. This ensures that the files are saved in two different locations, and since network servers are in turn backed up, your work is insured for a third time.

▶ Protecting your information

Your information needs to be protected from a variety of threats. These include:

- security
- virus infection
- adware
- spyware.

Security

The most obvious protection that you need is to ensure the confidentiality of your work. This can be achieved by limiting access to your files by the use of a password to prevent other people from accessing your work areas. Your college or university will provide you with a password to protect your files on its system, and you need to keep it safe and secure.

However, you need to decide if you want to protect your personal system with a password. If your computer is used by a range of people, you may need to ensure your work is protected from both deliberate and accidental damage. The Windows® operating system provides you with the means of establishing a password. You can create individual accounts for different users of the computer, and each account can have a separate password. To access this:

1. Select the Start button to reveal a menu of options.
2. Chose the Control Panel option to open a window with a series of options.
3. Select the User Accounts option. This provides access to the function to create a new account or change one.

Virus infection

It is now vital to protect your system from virus infection, which is a very real danger for any system that is connected to the Internet, or onto which files are transferred from floppy disks or other storage media. Your college will have extensive protection, but you need to install protection for your own system. There are several different products such as Norton AntiVirus. These need to be installed and set to check your system. The main choices are:

- to automatically check all your files and folders at regular intervals (such as once a week)
- to automatically check all e-mails that are received and sent
- to automatically check all new files
- to check floppy disks or other media
- to automatically update the information on new viruses (the system updates itself online so that it has the latest information).

Virus infection can be devastating and will cause you enormous problems. The best protection is prevention.

In addition to an antivirus system, you also need to take care how you operate the system. Some good practice is:

- Never open an e-mail attachment from a sender you do not know.
- Only download files from sites in which you have confidence (such as your university or college).

Adware and spyware

Viruses are not the only infection that can invade your system. Others are often called adware or spyware. These have various different effects, but one common consequence is that your system will slow down. Other effects are:

- to monitor your use of the World Wide Web
- to highjack your browser so that you are forced to visit certain sites
- to cause pop-ups to appear when you are surfing the Web.

Adware and spyware infect your system in similar ways to viruses. Antivirus software in some cases will not prevent infection. There are other special-purpose applications to remove or prevent adware and spyware infection (such as Ad-Ware Plus). These can be set in a similar way to antivirus software, and importantly need to be updated regularly online to ensure they are effective.

▶ Networks

College and university systems are based on networks, enabling students to use any computer within the institution. Your password and user name tells the system who you are and provides access to your files. Networks offer a potential to share resources with many users: for example, you can all use a range of printers. One useful approach is the shared folder, which is stored on one of the network servers (these are simply special-purpose computers), so that everyone in a particular group can access it. This shared folder can be for a particular course, or for a group of students working on a project together. You may be able to establish your own shared folders so that if you are collaborating with other students, resources can be pooled easily. Tutors will sometimes place documents relating to assignments, lecture notes, PowerPoint presentations, handouts and other information in a shared folder, so everyone can get a copy when he or she needs it.

A shared folder is accessed in a similar way to a folder on your own computer. The main difference is that the server will have a different drive letter from the ones on your own machine. On most personal computers you will be aware that C: is the internal hard disk and D: is the CD-Rom or DVD drive. On a server the letter could be G: or M: for example. You locate it by using the My Computer option available on the Windows desktop, or from the Start button in the same way you move to C:.

Top tips

1. **Help:** many computer users rarely use the help system provided by applications and the operating system, but it can save you time and quickly solve your problems.
2. **Managing files:** filing is an unglamorous subject, but being able to find a file is vital to the efficient use of a computer, and can save you time and frustration. The search facility is key to locating files when you need them.
3. **Security:** safeguarding your work from the many sources of attack (such as viruses) is critical. Understanding your virus protection is essential.
4. **Customizing the system:** the operating system provides you with the means of modifying your system to suit your personal needs.

▶ Summary

1.   Help: click on the Start button to reveal a window with the option Help and Support.
2.   Mouse properties: select the Control Panel and the Mouse option.
3.   Display: select the Control Panel and the Display option.
4.   Accessibility: select the Control Panel and the Accessibility option.
5.   Search: click the Start button to reveal a window with the option Search.
6.   Creating files and folders: highlight the All Programs option in the Start window to open a menu, highlight the Accessories option to open a sub-menu, then select the Windows Explorer option.

7.   Moving files and folders: highlight the chosen folder, and holding down the left mouse button, drag the folder to the new location before releasing it.

8.   Renaming files and folders: highlight the file or folder and select the File menu and the Rename option. Alternatively right-click on the file name to open a menu with the option Rename.

9.   Deleting files and folders: highlight the file or folder that you want to delete, then select the File menu and the Delete option.

10.   Individual accounts: select the Control Panel and the User Accounts option.

Glossary

Adobe Acrobat a file format that is widely used for documents presented on the Internet. Its file extension is .pdf (portable document format).

ADSL asymmetrical digital subscriber line, a high-speed telephone connection to the Internet.

adware a small software program which installs itself on a computer without the owner's permission and can undertake malicious activities such as monitoring users' use of the Internet.

asynchronous communication that does not require both the sender and receiver of the information to be online together (for example, e-mail is asynchronous).

backing up making a copy of files so that if anything goes wrong with the main system you have not lost your information.

blogging an online public diary.

Bluetooth a way of linking devices wirelessly.

bookmark marking a webpage so that you can locate it again. Browsers allow you to keep lists of bookmarks.

broadband a fast connection to the Internet from a computer.

cookies small software programs which attach themselves to a computer so that a website can recognize users.

dial-up a connection to the Internet through a standard telephone line.

domain part of a website address (its URL, or uniform resource locator).

downloading   transferring a file from a website to a computer.

driver   a software program designed to allow a computer device to work with an operating system.

encryption (*see also* PGP)   coding messages to safeguard their information.

field   (*see also* record and table) a single item of information in a database.

firewall   a security system to prevent unauthorized access to a computer when it is connected to the Internet.

firewire   a very quick way of transferring information to a computer.

FTP   file transfer protocol – the way files are moved around the Internet.

GIF   a graphics file format.

HTML   Hypertext Markup Language, a language used to construct websites.

HTTP   hypertext transfer protocol, controls access to information on websites.

hyphenation   dividing a word with a hyphen.

IP address   Internet protocol address, a number that identifies a computer as part of the Internet.

ISDN   integrated service digital network – a quick line to connect users to the Internet (but now being replaced by ADSL).

ISP   Internet Service Provider – the organization that provides users with a connection to the Internet.

JPEG   a graphics (picture) format used extensively on the Internet.

memory card   a small card on which a large amount of information can be stored. They are used in devices such as digital cameras to store pictures before transferring them to a computer.

Microsoft Reader   an application which allows users to read some electronic books (e-books).

moderator   the person who controls and monitors mailgroups to ensure that netiquette rules are followed. He or she will sometimes also act as a mentor.

netiquette   the rules of behaviour than hold in online environments (for example, how to behave in an e-mail discussion group).

open source   applications and operating systems that are provided with source code to allow users to customize them to their own needs.

pagination   control over where a page break will happen (to prevent related information being split across two pages).

patch   a software program designed to correct a problem (bug) in an application.

PGP   an encryption method.

plug-ins   small software programs which allow a browser to undertake additional functions such as viewing video images.

POP3   normally associated with an e-mail account, the system that allows users to access their e-mail from any location.

portal   a website that provides links to many other sites, usually with a common theme.

record   (*see also* field and table) a collection of fields relating to a common topic (such as the address of a building, street, town and postcode).

reference   position or location of a cell or range of cells in a spreadsheet.

replication   in a spreadsheet, copying is called replication in that formulas and functions will adjust to take account of their new position.

RTF   rich text format, a word processing format which is compatible with a wide range of applications.

screen reader   an application that reads aloud webpages so that visually impaired users can access the site.

search engine   an application that allows users to locate webpages across the World Wide Web or within a single site.

service pack   upgrades and bug fixes issued by software developers to enhance their products.

spam   essentially electronic junk mail.

spyware   small malicious programs that install themselves on a computer in order to monitor user activities.

streaming   a way of sending large volumes of information (such as video) across the Internet so that users can start to view it without having to wait until it is all downloaded.

synchronous   communication where both the sender and receiver of information need to be available at the same time (for example, a telephone conversation).

table (*see also* field and record)   a series of records (such as addresses of a group of friends).

Trojan   a program that pretends to be harmless while damaging a computer system.

unzip (*see also* zip)   to decompress a file so that it can be read by the application that created it.

URL   uniform resource locator, the address of a website.

USB   universal serial bus, a port which allows high-speed connections to peripheral devices.

virtual learning environment   an online facility that provides a variety of learning opportunities and facilities.

virus   a software program that can replicate itself onto a computer and vandalize a system (for example, by deleting important information).

widows and orphans   individual words (from the start or end of a paragraph) that are presented at the top or bottom of a page by the chosen formatting options. They can make a document appear unprofessional.

WiFi   wireless connectivity.

wiki   a website where users can add to and edit material on the site.

wizard   a system that provides assistance to users to undertake complex tasks by selecting from a range of options.

worm   another small program that can replicate itself and normally is harmful to a computer system.

zip (*see also* unzip)   to compress a file to reduce its size.

Further reading

Clarke, A. (2002) *New CLAIT Level One IT User Qualification Student Workbook*, Hodder and Stoughton.

Clarke, A. (2003) *CLAIT Plus Level Two IT User Qualification Student Workbook*, Hodder and Stoughton.

Clarke, A. (2004) *e-Learning Skills*, Palgrave Macmillan.

Index